Growing Up Gay In America

Informative and
practical advice
for teen guys
questioning their
sexuality and
growing up gay

Jason R. Rich

Published by:
Franklin Street Books
6750 SW Franklin Street, Suite A,
Portland, OR 97223. USA
(503) 968-6777

Author:
Jason R. Rich
email: jr7777@aol.com
www.Growing-Up-Gay.com

ISBN #: 0-97194140-8
First Edition - April 2002 (Revised July 2002)
Manufactured in the United States of America

This publication is designed to provide accurate and authoritative information with
regard to the subject matter covered. It is sold with the understanding that the
publisher and the author are not engaged in rendering legal, medical, psychological,
or other professional advice. If legal advice or other expert assistance is required, the
services of a competent professional person should be sought. Any references to a
product, service or organization do not constitute or imply an endorsement or
recommendation. The publisher and the author specifically disclaim any responsibility
for any liability, loss or risk (financial, personal or otherwise) which may be claimed or
incurred as a consequence, directly or indirectly, of the use and/or application of any
of the contents of this publication.

Certain terms mentioned in this book which are known or claimed to be trademarks or
service marks have been capitalized. Use of a term in this book should not be
regarded as affecting the validity of any trademark or service mark.

Table of Contents

Shout Out America

Q: What advice do you have for guys first coming out or coming to terms with their sexuality?

"It is very hard to come out. I am still having a hard time dealing with it. Once you do, there's no turning back, so think things through carefully."
- Alex, 23, McAllen, TX

"Know that you're not the only gay teenager out there. There are many other people that feel as afraid, depressed or confused as you do. Be yourself. It's much harder to try to be someone you're not."
- Josh, 18, Altanta, GA

"Don't get into a long-term relationship too early. Also, stay away from much older guys. They are everywhere and will want you just because you're young. Finally, always practice safe sex. Most importantly, have fun!"
- Dave, 28, South Beach, FL

"Just be yourself. If you know you're gay, bi or whatever, don't be scared!"
- Luke, 18, Erie, PA

"Be true to yourself. Don't try to 'fake it' by pursuing the opposite sex. Do without if you are uncomfortable. Involving a fake girlfriend in your cover-up and ultimately hurting her is tragic."
- Erik, 31, Altanta, GA

"Be honest with yourself and others. Also, be proud of yourself!"
- Joseph, 21, Windsor Locks, CT

"Don't be naive. Older and/or more experienced guys may try to take advantage of you sexually. Don't let them. Stay out of compromising positions and never get drunk with people you don't know."
- Aaron, 17, New York, NY

"Live it! Be it! Love it! Shape your life and personality based on your experiences. You'll learn a lot along the way. It's a long road, but be strong. You will survive! It's a wonderful life."
- Tristan, 19, Los Angeles

Introduction

As a teenager, you're probably filled with questions, strong emotions, raging hormones, a wide range of desires and countless challenges in your daily life. Well, guess what...that's normal!

But, have your sexual thoughts, urges and desires been focusing more on other guys as opposed to girls? Have you begun questioning your sexual orientation? Are you thinking perhaps you might be gay or bisexual, or that something is wrong with you?

As a result, are you confused, scared, lonely, or depressed because you're too embarrassed or ashamed to talk to others about what you're feeling and experiencing?

Whatever you're going through, be assured you're not alone! You're also ***not*** abnormal, a freak, a sexual deviant or "sick in the head" – no matter what people may tell you or what you might think.

It's common for young guys to be curious and/or experiment sexually. So, the feelings you're having don't automatically mean you're gay or even bisexual.

While there are no truly accurate statistics about the size of America's gay population, one estimate is that between five and six percent of America's youth (people under the age of 18) consider themselves to be gay, bisexual or lesbian. This translates to upwards of **2,700,000** young people in America who don't believe themselves to be straight.

If you do happen to be gay (or bisexual), do you truly understand what this means, or do you buy into the negative and incorrect stereotypes about homosexuality and the gay community? Try to keep an open mind as you begin to understand what you're feeling and experiencing.

In America, and throughout the world, people tend to be categorized into stereotypes. The less people know and understand about other people, the crueler and less accurate the stereotypes tend to be. Let's face it, being gay is something that most people don't understand, and many don't accept. This doesn't change the fact that one out of ten people in America is gay.

So, if you're gay, bisexual or still questioning your sexuality, you're not alone. This topic isn't something most teen guys choose to talk about openly, especially with straight friends, family members, religious leaders and teachers.

What Does It Mean To Be Gay?

Well, that's a tough question. The generic answer is that a guy who is *gay* is sexually attracted to other guys, not girls. Someone who is *bisexual* is attracted to both guys and girls. When it comes to discovering more about who you are, forget about titles and stereotypes.

Whether you're openly gay and have accepted yourself as being gay, or you're confused about your sexuality because of feelings you may have for other guys, it's common to feel alone, confused, scared and maybe even disgusted with yourself. Chances are, the concept of being gay goes against everything you've been taught and perhaps the religious or family values you've grown up with. Yet, you can't deny the thoughts, feelings, dreams and urges you have.

> A guy who is "gay" is primarily sexually attracted to other guys...**not** girls.

If you're currently questioning your sexuality, you're about to confront one of the scariest and confusing aspects of your life. While straight guys sometimes experiment with other guys, yet grow up to lead "straight" lives, there are certainly plenty of young guys, typically between the ages of 12 and 24, who know in their hearts they're gay or bisexual. They are forced to come to terms with who they are, and then decide whether or not they want to share this revelation with those around them. These days, young guys are realizing that they're gay very early in life, and many are coming out in their early teens.

Is Being Gay A Choice? Nope!

Most people don't wake up one morning and say, "Gee, being gay looks cool. I'm going to fall in love with a guy today and have sex by nightfall." Many people believe homosexuality is a choice... They're wrong! It's not typically a conscious decision to be gay or bisexual. Yet, there's no proof that being gay is hereditary (passed on through genes from your parents or grandparents). While you probably didn't choose to be gay, leading an openly gay life (where you come out to your friends and family, for example), is a decision you may or may not choose to make at this point in your life.

Someone who is comfortable with his sexuality and doesn't hide the fact he's gay is considered *openly gay*, while someone who keeps his sexual orientation and feelings a secret is considered to be *in the closet*. For someone who is gay, there are many misconceptions you'll need to deal with. There are also questions you'll need accurate answers to as you attempt to understand yourself, your feelings and your emotions.

While everyone's experience is unique, many gay guys face similar questions, issues and fears. Everyone has his own issues and fears to deal with and overcome. Unfortunately, this book can't supply you with all of the answers you need. Nor can it guarantee that no matter what your sexual preference is, your life will be happy and "normal." That's up to you!

What this book does offer, however, are answers to common questions; advice for dealing with many of the issues and situations you'll face as you confront your sexuality; and plenty of resources that will allow you to share your feelings, thoughts and fears with others who are in exactly the same situation.

Don't worry, you're not about to be preached to or lectured at in this book! What you'll read is advice and information from people who have been through or who are going through the exact same thing as you are right now.

Photo (c) 2002 Mark V. Lynch, Latent Images

If you learn nothing else from this book, you need to know that whatever you're going through, you're not alone! Even if you're afraid to discuss your sexuality openly at this point in your life, you can still communicate with others anonymously on the phone, online or through the mail. No matter how confused or scared you may be about the feelings, thoughts and urges you have, the trick to feeling better about yourself and building up your confidence is to communicate with others who understand your situation and who will support you.

Unfortunately, there are many people who simply don't understand or accept homosexuals. These people are homophobic and lack basic compassion and understanding. Not everyone, however, is homophobic. As you go through life, if you

Whether you realize it or not, millions of gay Americans lead happy, healthy and extremely successful lives.
There's nothing stopping you from becoming one of these people!

put in some effort, you'll be able to surround yourself with friends and loved ones who accept you, support you and care for you. It doesn't matter where you live, what ethnic background you come from or how much money you have. There are plenty of ways you can get the support you need and your questions answered!

Before you can expect others to accept you, the first step is to accept yourself. This book helps you come to terms with yourself as a person, then assists you in surrounding yourself with people who will support and accept you. *Growing Up Gay In America* provides you with the information you need to successfully overcome the obstacles you'll encounter at various points in your life.

The key to success is to face each obstacle and challenge with the right information – accurate information. Providing you with this needed practical information is the primary goal of this book.

In the past few years, the public's apparent acceptance and awareness of gays has increased. This has become apparent from popular television shows, like **The Real World, Dawson's Creek, Six Feet Under, Will & Grace, OZ** and **Queer As Folk**. These, and other shows like them, have gay-oriented storylines and characters, yet are watched and enjoyed by millions of mainstream (straight) Americans.

> Whatever's going through your mind right now, be patient, be open-minded and don't be afraid!

Despite what you see on these and other television shows, keep in mind that this is mostly fiction. While there is certainly a portion of the gay population that's into the club scene and that leads stereotypical sexually promiscuous lives (as sometimes depicted by several characters on **Queer As Folk**, for example), you don't have to be part of this group in order to be gay, nor do you have to become a cross-dresser, wear make-up, dress in tight-fitting clothing or become flamboyant.

Hey, you don't even need to listen to Madonna, Britney Spears or Barbara Streisand. As you'll soon discover, there are a growing number of support groups, magazines, books and resources (both online and in the real world) that you can anonymously take advantage of as you begin to explore your sexuality and understand what it means to be young and gay in America.

Gather the information you need, get your questions answered and then make whatever decisions are required for you to live the life you want to lead. If you truly want to be happy, you'll ultimately need to make the decisions that are right for you. Unfortunately, you can't rely on parents, friends, loved ones, religious leaders, doctors, psychologists or anyone else to make these decisions for you. Likewise, it's totally your decision as to who you share your thoughts, feelings and desires with.

> In this book, you'll discover how and where to meet other gay friends, how to deal with society's views on homosexuals, and how to deal with the various issues you're sure to encounter as you get older.

Each chapter of this book explores a different aspect of gay life and what it means to be gay and growing up in America. The first few chapters deal with issues, like determining whether or not you're actually gay; "coming out;" and dealing with your parents and relatives. If you are actually gay, much of what's in this book will help you live a safe, happy, healthy and prosperous life, develop relationships (yes, get a boyfriend), enjoy *safe* sex and plan for your future.

Simply by setting your hands on this book, you've taken a giant step toward better understanding what being young and gay (or bisexual) is all about.

Remember, no matter what your personal situation is, how scared, confused or depressed you might be, you're not alone!

This book will show you how you can easily find people who will understand and support you, who you can talk to (or communicate with), and who will assist you in overcoming whatever obstacles are in your way. Even if you choose to begin this personal journey on your own, this book will help you gather the courage and information you'll need and want.

In between each chapter, you'll see *Shout Out America* pages filled with quotes from teens (ages 15 to 25), just like you, from across America. These people have managed to come to terms with their sexuality and in many cases have overcome the challenges involved in coming out to friends and family. The advice and insight these people share is extremely valuable, as are the various other resources this book recommends.

Finally, while there's no shortage of psycho-babble, statistics and so-called "experts" who have opinions on what being gay is all about, you'll find very little of that stuff here. Instead, much of what you'll read comes directly from young people like yourself, from all over the country, who have firsthand experience growing up gay in America. It's from these people you can obtain a pretty accurate picture of what gay life is really all about and how wonderful being gay can actually be.

Jason R. Rich
email: jr7777@aol.com
www.Growing-Up-Gay.com

Chapter 1

Your Sexual Orientation

You know, the best way to deal with any of life's challenges, or to achieve a monumental goal, is to break apart what you're about to confront and focus on one piece at a time. It's true, admitting to yourself you're gay, then telling your friends, family, loved ones, coworkers, teachers and peers, for example, is a major decision that will probably have both positive and negative ramifications for the rest of your life.

However, if you pre-plan your approach, then focus on one aspect of the acceptance of your sexual orientation at a time, you'll find that what seemed like a monumental and impossible situation will begin to feel far more manageable.

As you've probably already figured out, there are many ramifications relating to the acceptance of your sexual orientation, if in fact, you are gay or bisexual. The questions you have need answers and the confusion and anxiety you may feel need to be alleviated.

If you are gay or bisexual, chances are, you've been having strange thoughts and feelings for a while, causing you to question your sexual orientation and identity.

As you move forward, don't jump into anything that could force you to become overwhelmed. Gather the information you need, come to terms with the issues you'll be dealing with, then take the appropriate actions when they become necessary (and once you've thought everything out).

As a teenager, you already have enough to deal with. Why compound the situation? Move forward at your own pace. Take each step as you're ready to proceed. Be brave and be proud of the person you are. Don't be afraid to love yourself and be loved by others. Just because your sexual orientation may be different, and at the moment, you have a secret, you're no less of a person and no less normal than anyone else.

This chapter focuses on you – who you are, what you believe to be true and your feelings. For the moment, forget about everyone else. Don't worry about what other people might think or say. For now, pay attention to your own needs, thoughts, desires, urges and concerns. Later, we'll deal with everyone else. Remember, focus on one issue at a time.

If you think you might be gay, bisexual or curious about other guys, that's okay. There's no need to freak out, panic or do anything rash. The first step is to clarify for yourself what you're feeling and thinking. Who are you as a person? That's the question you need to answer.

While you might not want to involve your friends or family at this time as you confront your sexuality (or what you think your sexuality might be), it's an excellent idea to find someone you **can** talk to, either in person, on the telephone or online. Find someone who understands your situation and who you can bounce ideas and questions off of.

Trust your instincts when it comes to choosing who you'll trust initially as you begin to explore your sexual identity and orientation.

If you're thinking about talking to a close friend or family member, for example, you might want to test the waters by bringing up homosexuality in a general conversation and seeing how the other person reacts. In this situation, however, people sometimes make derogatory (negative) comments about gays, because that's often what's perceived to be expected. Don't get turned off by this common reaction.

Rely on your instincts when it comes to choosing who you'll trust as you initially begin to explore your sexual identity and orientation.

Later in this chapter, as well as throughout this book, you'll find contact information for people who you can talk to (anonymously, if you wish) in order to gather more information and calm your fears. Of course, if you have a brother, sister, close friend, relative, teacher, guidance counselor or someone else you truly trust, that's an excellent person to talk to. If you have a gay relative or know someone at school who is openly gay, for example, these might also be people worth chatting with.

It's true, talking to someone for the first time about an extremely private and personal issue, such as your sexuality, is very scary. After all, you're probably worried about what will happen if the person you choose to trust and confide in reacts negatively to what you have to say. As you'll discover, there are several steps you can take to alleviate this fear. For example, spend a bit of time evaluating the best person to talk to. Based on your own personal situation, the person or people you choose to confide in will vary.

No matter what, you can always dial a toll-free number and make contact with a support organization, such as The Trevor Project Hotline, which will provide someone for you to speak with (anonymously, if you choose).

It's important to understand that no matter how scared and alone you feel, in reality, you're not alone and there's no reason to deal by yourself with the emotions you're feeling. If you're feeling scared, alone, frustrated or depressed, find someone – anyone – to talk to.

Throughout this book, you'll find a handful of free resources you can take advantage of in order to gather the support you want and the answers you need.

Some of these organizations include:

Parents, Families & Friends of Lesbians & Gays (PFLAG)

PFLAG is a national, non-profit organization with more than 80,000 members and supporters, plus more than 460 affiliates in the United States. There are local chapters of PFLAG located across America. To find a local chapter, visit the organization's Web site at **www.pflag.org**, or call the group's national office in Washington, D.C. at **(202) 467-8180**.

Attending a local PFLAG meeting in your area is an excellent way to meet other teenagers who are questioning their sexuality or who have already come out as being gay or bisexual.

Parents of gay teenagers also attend these meetings and can provide insight and support when it comes to sharing the information with your own parents. It's not necessary to be gay or bisexual to attend a PFLAG meeting, and there's no charge.

The Travor Project Hotline

No matter what time of the day or night it is, if you're scared, depressed, lonely or suicidal, call this toll-free phone number and talk to someone who cares about you and who wants to help.

Call toll-free from any telephone - **(800) 850-8078 / www.thetrevorproject.org**. This is the first round-the-clock national toll-free suicide hotline for gay and questioning youth. It's open 24 hours a day, seven days a week, 365 days a year. Teens with nowhere else to turn can talk openly to trained counselors, find local resources and take important steps toward becoming healthy adults. All calls are *free* and *confidential*.

The Gay & Lesbian National Hotline

This is another free telephone resource. From any telephone (including public pay phones or cell phones), call **(888) THE-**

GLNH (888-843-4564) and speak with a trained volunteer who understands and can help you cope with any situation pertaining to your sexuality.

According to this organization, "Many times a young person just coming out has nowhere to turn for help or guidance. Having a trained and compassionate volunteer who knows how to listen can make a tremendous difference at such a critical juncture in their lives. Similarly, the stress and anxiety that many HIV positive and negative people alike are faced with can be greatly reduced by the support that the Gay & Lesbian National Hotline will provide.

"In addition, the Gay & Lesbian National Hotline maintains a database of over 17,000 local community groups, organizations, businesses and professionals. One of the most important steps in keeping our [gay] community strong is to keep our community connected. The Hotline helps provide that connection by linking callers with the thousands of services that are available to them."

This free hotline is available Monday through Friday, from 4:00pm until midnight, and on Saturdays, from noon until 5:00pm (East Coast time).

The Kristin Brooks Hope Center

This organization offers a toll-free number (**800-SUICIDE**) for people who are depressed or suicidal. The Kristin Brooks Hope Center has also created a unique web site (**www.livewithdepression.org**) that gives you a raw, personal glimpse into depression and how it affects those around you. In addition, you will find a clear, step-by-step path to follow out of the darkness caused by depression. "There is hope and you can feel happy again," reports the organization.

You're Not Alone!
Here's How To Find Proof For Yourself!

It's easy to read in a book, "Don't worry, you're not alone! Everything will be okay!" Well, reading those words and believing them are two very different things, especially if you feel alone and isolated, with nobody to talk to about what's going through your head. The reality is, you're really not alone!

There are millions of gay teenagers in America and throughout the world. Plus, there are millions of gay adults who have already questioned their sexuality and who experienced what you're going through right now.

Making contact with other gay people will be extremely helpful to you, especially if you're feeling alone and/or confused.

Making contact with other gay people will be extremely helpful to you, especially if you're feeling alone and/or confused.

It doesn't matter which of the following options you choose. The goal is to learn about and meet other gay (and bisexual) people you can openly communicate with.

To prove to yourself that you're not alone in what you're experiencing, try any of the following suggestions today... Why wait?

■ Go online to Gay.com (**www.gay.com**) and use the chat feature, or visit one of the many other Web sites targeted to the gay community. If you have access to the Internet, you can anonymously chat online with other people of all ages, in your area or anywhere in the world, who are gay, bisexual or questioning their sexuality. America Online also offers chat rooms filled with people you can chat with virtually anytime, day or night. Meeting and interacting with other gay people online can be extremely comforting. It's also a way to safely meet other gay people who you might eventually interact with in-person. To learn more about how to chat live with other gay or bisexual people online, check out Chapter 7.

■ Attend a PFLAG meeting in your area. This option isn't anonymous, but the people attending the support group meeting will be very understanding. Plus, you'll see firsthand that there are other gay and bisexual young people who are going through (or who have gone through) exactly what you're experiencing now. In-person interaction with other gay people is extremely valuable and comforting, especially in this type of supportive environment.

■ Call a gay youth support organization.

■ Go to a large newsstand (or a bookstore, such as Barnes & Noble or Borders, that sells magazines) and pick up a copy of *XY* magazine. This is an awesome, non-pornographic magazine written specifically for gay teen guys. In addition to informative articles, you'll find plenty of photos of hot, young, often shirtless guys. You might also want to pick up copies of *Out* or *The Advocate* magazine.

■ Talk to someone who you know is gay (someone at school, a relative or someone in your community). Developing a nonsexual friendship with an adult gay man can be an incredible source of support. In addition to being a friend, this type of individual might also act as a mentor in other aspects of your life, besides helping your come to terms with your sexual orientation. Don't be afraid to learn from the experiences of others.

■ If you're over the age of 18 (21 in some situations), consider going to a gay club in your city. Or, if there is a "gay area" in your city, like West Hollywood (California), Key West

(Florida), various parts of San Francisco (California) or Provincetown (Massachusetts), go visit and spend time there. While this can be scary at first, you'll probably begin to feel more at ease with yourself when you're surrounded by openly gay people.

- Attend the annual 'Gay Day' at Disney World (Orlando, Florida) or Disneyland (Anaheim, California). These events are not sanctioned by The Walt Disney Company, but they attract thousands of young gay people from throughout the country. Other theme parks around the country also host similar events. For details, visit the Gay Day Web site at **www.gayday.com**.

- Attend a Gay Pride event in your city. Most medium-to-large size cities now host annual Gay Pride events. The Interpride Web site (**www.interpride.org**) is one resource for finding the dates and locations for these events worldwide.

To find the gay or "mixed" clubs in your city, one resource is DigitalCity.com (**www.digitalcity.com**). Once you choose your city, use the 'Search' feature and enter the words 'gay clubs.'

What Is Sexual Orientation?

Some people classify being gay as a 'sexual preference.' This is a bogus term. It suggests that a gay person is gay by choice (i.e., it's their preference). If you're gay, you already know it isn't a choice.

It's far more accurate to describe being gay or bisexual as a sexual orientation. What exactly does this term mean, however? Here's what some of the experts (you know, the shrinks) have to say:

According to The American Psychological Association (APA), "Sexual Orientation is an enduring emotional, romantic, sexual or affectional attraction to another person. It is easily distinguished from other components of sexuality including biological sex, gender identity (the psychological sense of being male or female) and the social gender role (adherence to cultural norms for feminine and masculine behavior)....Sexual orientation is different from sexual behavior because it refers to feelings and self-concept. Persons may or may not express their sexual orientation in their behaviors."

Photo (c) 2002 Mark V. Lynch, Latent Images

As to what impacts someone's sexual orientation, the APA states, "There are numerous theories about the origins of a person's sexual orientation; most scientists today agree that sexual orientation is most likely the result of a complex interaction of environmental, cognitive and biological factors. In most people, sexual orientation is shaped at an early age. There is also considerable recent evidence to suggest that biology, including genetic or inborn hormonal factors, play a significant role in a person's sexuality."

Thus, based on everything science dictates so far (plus the experience of millions of gay people from around the world), human beings can not choose to be either gay or straight.

While being gay isn't a choice, how you act as a gay person is entirely up to you.

There is no "cure" for being gay. There's only acceptance or denial. Seeking out therapy can not and will not change your sexual orientation.

Many gay and bisexual people, however, choose to pursue some form of therapy to assist them in dealing with the stress of coming to terms with their sexuality, or coming out, for example.

The APA reports, "Even though most homosexuals live successful, happy lives, some homosexual or bisexual people may seek to change their sexual orientation through therapy, often coerced by family members or religious groups to try and do so. The reality is that homosexuality is not an illness. It does not require treatment and is not changeable."

Not all of the gay and bisexual people who seek help from a mental health professional want to change their sexual orientation. Some people seek out psychological help in dealing with the coming out process, or for developing strategies to deal with prejudice. Gays also face many of the same stresses and challenges as straight people and seek assistance in dealing with those issues, just as straight people do.

"Sexual orientation emerges for most people in early adolescence without any prior sexual experience. Although we can choose whether to act on our feelings, psychologists do not consider sexual orientation to be a conscious choice that can be voluntarily changed," reports the APA.

There is no need to be embarrassed about working with a mental health professional who can assist you in dealing with your personal challenges. These people can provide comfort, stability and a wealth of knowledge, in a casual and nonthreatening environment.

Coming To Terms With Your Own Sexuality

On the surface, you might think that determining your sexual orientation is an easy, straightforward thing. In reality, for many people, especially teens, it's not. This chapter is going to explain some of the labels or buzzwords, like "gay," "straight," "bisexual" and "transgender" and help you determine how these terms may apply to you.

Keep in mind, not everyone fits nicely into one of these categories. In fact, it's pretty typical for all teen guys to at one point or another question their sexuality and perhaps even experiment with a same-sex partner.

> Simple curiosity or experimentation seldom means you're actually gay or even bisexual.

Throughout your teen years, you're going to experience many changes. Your physical body will change, your urges will change, you'll become more independent, you'll become smarter, your relationship with your family will evolve and you'll begin to develop your own set of interests. Without taking into account your sexuality, you'll be faced with challenges at school, at home and with your peers. You'll also have to deal with your hormones and heightened sexual urges. If you are, in fact, gay or bisexual, this is one period of your life when things could get a bit confusing.

Being gay is neither an abnormality or an illness. It's simply a fact of life, like your height, skin color or ethnic background.

As you undergo these various life changes, understand that your feelings and experiences are all normal, even if they're not the same as what your friends are experiencing.

If you're like most teenagers, you're probably already uncomfortable with your looks, your weight, your height and/or your complexion, for example. Perhaps you have some other insecurities relating to your appearance. While having confusing thoughts about your sexuality will lead to additional anxiety, there's no reason why you can't confront these feelings and deal with them (whether or not you choose to share what you're experiencing with those around you).

At this point, little is known about what actually causes a guy to be gay or bisexual. Whatever the reason is, it's important to understand that the feelings you have, even if you've been taught by others that they're abnormal or wrong, aren't your fault. These are feelings you have little or no control over, and there is nothing wrong with them.

No matter what's going through your head, be aware that neither the American Psychological Association nor the American Psychiatric Association consider homosexuality to be an emotional or mental disorder. People from every ethnic group, religion, economic background, financial background, race, religion and from places all over the world are gay.

Likewise, there is no direct correlation between someone who is gay and his upbringing, even if that upbringing included abuse (physical, mental or sexual). While some people who were abused in some way are gay (or bisexual), plenty of others are heterosexual, which means there is little or no correlation between mental or physical abuse and sexual orientation.

So, since being gay isn't a physical or mental disease, it can't be cured – mainly because there is

> Neither the American Psychological Association nor the American Psychiatric Association consider homosexuality to be an emotional or mental disorder.

nothing to cure. According to the American Psychological Association, no scientific evidence exists to support the effectiveness of any therapies that attempt to convert homosexuals into heterosexuals (gays into straights).

Many gay guys "discover" their sexuality for certain as they mature and experience puberty. Instead of naturally being attracted to girls, their sexual desires and thoughts focus on guys.

If you're truly straight, experimenting with a guy won't make you gay or even bisexual. Likewise, if you're gay, trying to force yourself to be sexually attracted to a female will prove difficult, if not impossible.

Despite everything you might have heard, being gay (or bisexual) isn't something that you catch (like a common cold or disease), get recruited into or can be taught.

If, in your heart, you believe you have more than a passing curiosity about other guys, you could be gay or bisexual, which as you'll soon discover, isn't the end of the world. For the moment, don't jump to any conclusions about yourself or what the ramifications of being gay or bisexual might mean should you decide to act on your feelings or allow anyone else to find out.

First, let's focus on the various buzzwords and define their meanings. Even once you understand these terms, don't be surprised if you don't consider yourself to fit nicely into a category. Putting a title on your sexuality isn't important.

What's far more critical is that you develop an understanding of yourself, come to terms with who you are and what you feel and ultimately become comfortable with what you perceive your sexual orientation to be.

Popular Terms and Their Meanings

- 'Gay' or 'homosexual' describes a guy who is sexually interested in other guys (not girls). There are many terms that are derogatory used to describe someone who is gay, like 'fag,' 'faggot,' 'queen,' 'homo,' 'fudge packer' or 'queer.'
- 'Bisexual' refers to someone who is sexually attracted to both guys and girls.
- A 'curious' or 'questioning' guy doesn't yet truly understand his own sexuality and is open to the idea of experimenting with people of the same sex.
- A 'transvestite' is a male who chooses to dress in women's clothing. This has been described by some as a psychological condition. In many cases, a transvestite is straight, but enjoys wearing women's clothing.
- A 'drag queen' is a guy who dresses in women's clothing for show, typically to perform. You'll often find drag queens 'performing' at gay clubs.
- Someone who is a 'transsexual' is in the process of converting (or has converted) from being a male (physically and mentally) to a female, through surgery. He wants to live his life as a female.
- 'Straight' or 'heterosexual' guys are sexually attracted to girls and have no sexual interest in guys. Gay people often refer to straights jokingly as 'breeders.'
- Someone who is 'closeted' (or 'in the closet') is a gay (or bisexual) person who tries to hide his sexuality.
- A gay person who doesn't hide or lie about his sexual orientation is referred to as being 'openly gay' or 'out.'
- When someone is 'outed,' his sexual orientation is publicly revealed, typically against his will.

You Can Control Your Actions!

Having urges, desires or sexual feelings toward someone (a guy or a girl) doesn't mean you're forced to act upon them. There are plenty of people who have gay tendencies but choose to lead straight lives and never act on their feelings or desires. This is often because the public perception of homosexuality in America is negative. Nobody wants to be in the minority and disliked or misunderstood by others. Likewise, many organized religions frown upon or outright disapprove of homosexuality, which frightens people into believing they'll be condemned to hell, for example, if they pursue their natural sexual desires.

There are countless arguments that can be made as to why someone should or shouldn't admit to and come to terms with his sexual feelings and orientation. As for the religious aspects of this decision, that's something you need to deal with on your own, based on your personal beliefs, and perhaps with the guidance of a religious leader who is open-minded and understanding.

Later in this book, you'll discover many resources you can utilize to help you come to terms with the religious ramifications of being gay or bisexual. Ultimately, however, it must be your own internal belief system that dictates your choices and the paths you choose to pursue, even if this means going against the wishes of your parents, friends, teachers, coworkers and/or religious leaders.

For someone to be truly at peace and happy, most people believe that it's important to come to terms with and accept yourself for the person you are. Sure, if you're overweight you can go on a diet. However, if you're truly gay, little or nothing can be done to convert you into being straight, just like you can't control your height, skin color or ethnic background. You can, however, learn to accept who you are and lead a happy and productive life, whether or not you choose to come out of the closet and disclose your sexual orientation to others.

Gay? Don't Jump To Conclusions!

If you're questioning your sexuality because you have a strong emotional or sexual attraction toward a same-sex friend; you're curious about what gay life is all about; you think a guy you know is hot and you develop a crush; or perhaps you've had a sexual dream that involved another guy, this doesn't necessarily mean you're gay or even bisexual, especially if on an ongoing basis you find yourself attracted to girls.

Likewise, if you've already had one or two sexual experiences with a guy (maybe you were drunk or just plain curious), or you became aroused during a physical examination by a doctor; during a massage by a male masseur; while wrestling around with a male friend; or in the locker room after a team practice or gym class, this does not automatically mean you're gay.

When most guys who are openly gay look back at their feelings before they came to terms with their sexuality, they come to see that starting at a young age (or when puberty kicked in), they had thoughts, feelings or urges for other guys, in addition to or instead of having similar feelings for girls (like their peers). In other words, they somehow felt "different" from the other kids, which is something that's hard to define in words, but if you feel (or have felt) it, you'll understand.

It must be your own internal belief system that dictates your choices and the paths you choose to pursue, even if this means going against the wishes of your parents, friends, teachers, coworkers and/or religious leaders.

Sure, you can go into a self-imposed state of denial and try to convince yourself you're straight. However, if in your heart you know you might be gay or bisexual, these are feelings and thoughts you should confront, deal with and, if necessary, come to terms with. Even if you don't want to admit what you're feeling to anyone else just yet, don't try to hide your feelings from yourself.

> Just because you might be gay (or bisexual), there's no need to adopt what's commonly believed to be a stereotypical gay lifestyle.

Be honest with yourself! In reality, most of what comes to mind when someone thinks about a stereotypical gay person has little or nothing to do with the life a typical homosexual person actually leads. After all, there is no single gay lifestyle, just as there is no single straight lifestyle.

Many gay people don't come close to fitting into the common gay stereotype from a physical, personality or mental standpoint. There's so much more to being gay than sex, being flamboyant or acting effeminate.

Likewise, for most people, being gay relates to their sexual orientation, but has little or no impact on their otherwise perfectly normal day-to-day activities.

If you're pondering what your sexual orientation actually is, to help clarify the situation, ask yourself questions, and be totally honest with yourself when you think about the answers.

Here are some questions to think about:

■ When you dream, daydream or fantasize about sex (as you masturbate, for example), do you think about guys or girls?

■· Have you ever had a crush on or been in love with another guy, such as a best friend, a cute boy in your class, a teacher or your coach?

- In general, do you think you're different from the other guys you know and hang around with?

Admitting to yourself that you're gay or bisexual doesn't mean you are required in any way to change your life habits or lifestyle!

You Can Lead a Totally Happy Life, Even If You're Gay!

Gay people hold regular jobs, have regular hobbies and do many of the same things that heterosexual people do. Unfortunately, admitting to yourself (and to others) that you're gay isn't easy. As a result, those who choose to stay closeted can lead lonely and unhappy lives, mainly because of fear of what others will think. There are many ways gay people can come to terms with their sexuality. After accepting themselves, they can make an effort to surround themselves with accepting friends and family members, for example, who support them, even if others don't.

If you play sports, have a job or enjoy spending time with friends, all those aspects of your life can stay the same. Adopting a gay lifestyle, however, may mean that you won't get married (to a woman) and have children in the traditional sense, but you could eventually develop a lifelong relationship with another man and have a close and loving family of your own. Chapter 8 explores this aspect of living as a gay adult.

Forget about the misconceptions and misinformation you might already have. For example, being gay doesn't automatically mean you're going to catch HIV/AIDS and die at a young age. AIDS is a deadly virus that gay, bisexual and straight men (and women) can catch as a result of participating in unsafe (unprotected) sex with someone who is already infected; using and/or sharing dirty drug needles; or in very rare cases, through a blood transfusion (when you're given infected blood during surgery). Due to extensive testing, this latter scenario virtually never happens anymore. Finally, women who are infected with HIV/AIDS can transmit the disease to an unborn child during pregnancy.

Plenty of gay men are involved in loving relationships with other men and lead long and happy (AIDS-free) lives. Yes, AIDS is certainly a concern among the gay community. However, being careful and always practicing safe sex are ways to prevent catching HIV/AIDS. There's a lot more to understand about this topic, so be sure to check out Chapter 6.

One of the biggest questions people have when they begin to explore their sexuality and think about the possibility they might be gay, is whether or not the people around them (friends, family, etc.) will accept them. Well, step one is to accept yourself.

The simple answer to the question, however, about others accepting you, is that some people will accept you right away, while others won't. Several other chapters in this book deal with coming out to and being accepted by your parents, friends, peers, teachers, coworkers and other people you encounter in your day-to-day life.

It's perfectly normal and common for a gay or bisexual teenager to determine his sexuality but not go public with the information for several months or years. In the meantime, he might gather information and make gay friends online, for example. Yes, in a sense this is leading two distinct lives, which isn't typically a good idea, but if it works for you on a temporarily basis, that's what is important.

Plenty of gay men are involved in loving relationships with other men and lead long and happy (AIDS-free) lives.

Wait Until You're Ready!

Remember, you need to do what makes you feel comfortable, without worrying about what other people think or how they might react. Whatever you do, don't come out to the public until you're ready. Everyone is different and has his own timeline for dealing with these issues. Some guys know in their heart they're gay and come out when they're 15 or 16. Others wait until they're in their late-twenties or in their thirties before they truly come to terms with their sexual orientation and are honest about it to themselves and others.

There are important reasons why you should ultimately come out to those you're close to, once you come to terms with your own sexuality. Mainly, it's best to have relationships with friends and family that are based on truth, openness and honesty. If you're hiding the fact you're gay with those close to you, you're keeping a pretty big secret.

At the same time, there are many reasons why you might want to keep your sexuality a secret, at least at this point in your life, especially if you're convinced that the people around you won't be understanding, accepting and supportive. Coming out to those around you can be risky. Not to scare you, but the reality is, you could be

Photo (c) 2002 Mark V. Lynch, Latent Images

rejected by people you truly care about. There are ways, as you'll soon discover, to greatly limit the potential risk of rejection.

Only by weighing the pros and cons can you make an intelligent decision about coming out. Coming out to those around you is different, however, than meeting new gay friends online or in person, then exploring and learning about your sexuality with the help of these people. If you choose to tell people, begin by confiding in the people you're most comfortable sharing this personal information with. This may be close friends, family members or the people you talk to on a support hotline or meet at a gay support group.

Talk To Someone You Trust

Choosing to keep your feelings to yourself for the time being is fine. However, staying in the closet and not talking to anyone for a long time can cause you to become stressed and unhappy. Thus, you might choose to reveal or explore your sexuality with people you meet online or through various support groups first.

Later, you could try talking to someone who is already in your life – and who could ultimately become part of your personal support system.

Aside from people you meet online or through support groups, listed alphabetically below are ideas for people you might want to be open and honest with as you explore your sexuality:

- Brother or sister
- Close friend
- Doctor / physician / nurse
- Parents or grandparents
- Relative
- Religious leader (Keep in mind, some organized religions frown upon homosexuality, so unless the person you confide in is open-minded, you might want to look elsewhere for positive support, before you deal with the religious ramifications of your sexuality based on your religious beliefs)
- School guidance counselor
- Someone who is openly gay in your community

- Teacher / college professor
- Therapist

One of the benefits of talking with a doctor or a therapist is that they're obligated to keep whatever you discuss confidential, unless they believe you're going to harm yourself or someone else.

Dealing With Depression

Depression is often a side effect of being confused about your sexuality, especially if you also feel lonely and scared. If you begin to feel depressed for more than a few days, it's important to take positive steps to identify the cause of your depression and find a way to overcome it.

Depression can have a negative impact on all aspects of your life. Just because you're depressed, however, it doesn't mean you need to be taking strong antidepressant medications (prescribed by a doctor).

Simply by talking about your feelings, eating well, getting plenty of sleep, participating in activities you enjoy and exercising, many of the symptoms of your depression may diminish or disappear. You might also choose to start a diary and write down your feelings on paper (or use a word processor). You can keep your writings totally private, but this exercise might help you confront and understand the feelings you're experiencing, plus figure out a way to deal with them.

If you're depressed for an extended period of time, seek out help and talk to a doctor, therapist, guidance counselor, parent or a friend.

It's common for teenagers (straight, bisexual or gay) to experience periods of depression. Being depressed for days, weeks or months at a time, however, is different from being in a bad mood.

To counteract your depression, don't turn to alcohol or drugs. While this may sound cliché, these substances are dangerous, addictive and will only mess you up more. Don't hide or run away from your problems by trying to escape through drugs and alcohol. This approach does **not** work! Sure, it takes more energy and a stronger will to confront your depression and fears (and their underlying causes), but the long-term outcome will be much better.

There are many possible causes of depression. Ongoing stress is just one cause that people questioning their sexuality encounter. If you're experiencing one or more of the following symptoms, talking to someone, such as a therapist, might be extremely beneficial. If you're dealing with intense feelings of depression, the worst thing you can do is try to deal with the situation by yourself. Even if you're not ready to discuss your sexuality, you should still talk to someone immediately about your depression.

Symptoms of Depression

- Thoughts of death keep popping into your head and perhaps consuming your thoughts. You feel like you have no future and you're destined to remain unhappy for the rest of your life.
- You are experiencing a loss of interest in normal daily activities, including things you used to really enjoy.
- You're experiencing a reduced interest in sex or your sex drive is greatly diminished.
- You're experiencing an overall sad or depressed mood resulting in feeling hopeless, helpless or having the need to cry.

- You're experiencing significant weight loss or weight gain. You have no appetite or you're eating too much.
- You're having trouble thinking, concentrating and making decisions.
- You're not sleeping well or you sleep too much due to an ongoing lack of energy.
- You're suffering from low self-esteem or feel guilty about the thoughts you're having (relating to your sexuality, for example).

Find A Therapist You Can Trust

If you need to speak with a therapist, you can do so without your family and friends knowing. Even if your parents know you're seeing a therapist, however, what you discuss with the therapist will remain 100 percent confidential. Thus, you'll want to find a therapist who you trust, who you can relate to (and who relates to you) and who you feel comfortable with. If you have health insurance, the costs of seeing a therapist is often totally covered. There are also therapists who work for free. You can typically find these people through referrals from gay support groups or your school's guidance counselor.

When choosing your therapist, you can decide if your therapist will be a male or female. To get the most out of speaking with a therapist, however, you need to be open and honest, plus give the therapy sessions a chance to work. One or two meetings won't provide instant solutions.

Find a therapist who will listen to you. If you meet with a therapist and all they want to do is put you on antidepressants, without listening to what you have to say, find someone else. If you're feeling depressed, scared or alone, you need someone to talk to immediately. Seek out help; there's absolutely nothing to be ashamed of!

If you're gay (or bisexual) and depressed, you're certainly not alone. Unfortunately, the statistics relating to gay teenagers and depression, suicide and drug/alcohol abuse are staggering and extremely scary. You, however, don't have to be a statistic!

Simply by reading this book, you've already proven to yourself you have the strength to come to terms with and accept what you're experiencing. Now, if you're feeling scared or depressed, you need to summon the courage and strength to seek out the support and love you need. Call a toll-free support hotline, speak with a friend, attend a support group – but don't hide your anxiety and depression in drugs or alcohol.

The ability to communicate with other gay people, through email and online chat rooms is an incredible resource, especially if you live in a rural area where openly gay people don't exist (at least to your knowledge).

Whether you believe it or not, in terms of dealing with your sexuality, your teen years are by far the hardest. Things do get much easier and better, especially if you take the basic steps necessary to take control of your life and be happy. Trying to get through this part of your life alone, however, isn't the answer.

So, You Think You Might Be Gay?

Has anything you've read thus far hit home? Are you starting to think that the thoughts you have about guys may be more than a passing phase?

Well, if so, the good news is, you're brave enough to face the truth about your sexual orientation and, hopefully, you're willing to open your mind enough to accept it. You're well on your way to leading the happy and productive life you've dreamed about. Being true to yourself is the first step.

By opening yourself up to the possibility that you are gay or bisexual, you're giving yourself permission to learn, explore, expand your horizons and ultimately reach your true potential.

Once you're honest with yourself and acknowledge and accept your desires and feelings, the next positive step forward is to learn about what being gay really means. If you have access to the Internet, you have at your fingertips the most powerful information resource is the world. You can research issues and facts about homosexuality, communicate with other people who are gay and safely (and, if you choose, anonymously) explore your sexuality.

Of course, you can also access the tremendous amount of gay pornography on the Internet and see, for example, if hot naked guys and/or sexual images of guys having sex with other guys actually turns you on.

Simply reading about being gay isn't a total solution. It's a beginning. Meeting and interacting in-person with other people who are gay, especially others your own age, will make coming to terms with your sexuality much easier. It's also an opportunity to explore possible romantic interests, date and, perhaps at some point, when you're ready, be sexually intimate with another male. But once again, don't rush into anything! Start off by learning what it means to be gay.

Discover what the obstacles are you'll need to overcome if you choose to come out and be openly gay in your community. Find out how to practice safe sex and what risks are involved when you're sexually intimate with other guys. At this point, reading and interacting with other members of the gay community is an excellent starting point as you begin to come to terms with your own sexual orientation.

While keeping your current circle of friends, make new (gay or bisexual) friends you can trust. Developing a close circle of friends - who you care about, can depend on and trust - will make your life richer and happier. Friends can become as close as family members, and true friendships can last a lifetime. If you don't already have friends who fit this description, make an effort to find some. If you already have close friends, chances are that when you're ready, they'll accept your sexuality, just as they currently accept you as a friend right now.

In some ways, meeting gay friends is easier than meeting straight friends, because when you enter into an online gay-oriented chat room, visit a gay club or café, or attend a gay support group meeting (such as a PFLAG meeting), for example, the people you'll interact with all have something pretty major in common. Shared experiences are a foundation for friendship. While it's easier said than done, don't allow self-doubt or fear to hold you back from making friends, learning what being gay really means and learning more about yourself.

It's time to take the initiative, be brave and whether or not you choose to be openly gay, learn how to be proud of the person you are. In the process, try to discover what your likes and dislikes are.

As you embark on this personal journey and quest for knowledge don't, however, lose focus on the other aspects of your life. If you're a skilled athlete, musician, artist, a good student or someone who does volunteer work, for example, stay actively involved in the activities you enjoy. Focus on being a good student, a loving family member, a responsible son, a trusting friend and a good citizen in your community. Whatever your long-term goals are, pursue them with a passion.

Being gay doesn't have to be a hindrance to achieving whatever it is you want to succeed at!

Youth Guardian Services
www.youth-guard.org

If you're not yet ready to come out to your family and friends, or even attend a support group meeting in person, Youth Guardian Services is an online support center for gay, bisexual and questioning teens. The best thing about this free service is that people interact directly with each other through email lists.

Depending on how old you are and what your situation is, you'll find a forum for you to exchange ideas, ask questions and interact with people your own age, who are going through exactly what you're going through right now.

According to the organization, "The YOUTH E-mail Lists are a group of email mailing lists separated by age groups (13 to 17, 17 to 21, 21 to 25). The goal of these lists is to provide gay, lesbian, bisexual, transgendered and questioning youth an open forum to communicate with other youth. The content ranges from support topics in times of crisis, to "chit-chat" and small talk. Each list is operated by a volunteer staff who are in the same age group as the list subscribers."

This Web site also offers a directory of local gay friendly counselors, therapists, psychologists, psychiatrists and other mental health professionals, plus detailed information about gay friendly colleges and universities.

Photo (c) 2002 Mark V. Lynch, Latent Images

Shout Out America
Q: What was it that made you sure you were gay?

"There was a boy in my class that I was attracted to. I realized that it was an attraction I'd never had toward a girl. I was 11 at the time."
- Michael, 21, Ft. Lauderdale, FL

"I think I was around seven-years-old. I knew I just wasn't attracted to girls. Now I'm 16, and I have not yet come out to the people close to me."
- Mike, 16, Sparks, NV

"When I was 14 or 15, I figured out I didn't want a girl-friend. What I really wanted was a boyfriend. I didn't act upon these feelings until just before my 17th birthday."
- Josh, 18, Atlanta, GA

"I was very little. I went from wanting to be a girl when I was little to liking guys."
- Kyle, 18, Boulder, CO

"I'd see pictures of hot guys in magazines when I was 15 or so, and get aroused. I'd also keep check-ing out the guys in the locker room at school. I knew I was different then."
- Chris, 21, New York, NY

"I was 16. I stopped being sexually attracted to my girl-friend and starting thinking about guys in her place."
- Tristan, 19, Los Angeles, CA.

"When I was 16, I totally fell head-over-heels in love with my best friend. I actually came out when I was 19."
- Bryan, 22, Orlando, FL

Now, That's Entertainment
Gay-Oriented TV Shows and Magazines

One way to learn more about homosexuality is to see how it's depicted on television as well as in magazines. Aside from the countless gay pornography magazines on the newsstand, you'll find several news and entertainment-oriented magazines actually designed to be read for the articles.

TV Shows with Gay Themes and/or Characters

- Dawson's Creek (WB)
- OZ (HBO)
- Queer As Folk (Showtime)
- Real Sex (HBO / CineMax)
- Six Feet Under (HBO)
- The Real World (MTV)
- Will & Grace (NBC)

Gay-Oriented Magazines Worth Reading
(Available online, at newsstands and bookstores)

- **Genre (www.genremagazine.com)** - A general interest, gay-oriented magazine for all ages.
- **Instinct (www.instinctmag.com)** - Great pictures, great articles, great for teen and adult guys alike.
- **Out (www.out.com)** - Another extremely well-written and informative gay-oriented magazine for guys of all ages. Read about entertainment, fashion, current events and more. (Great pictures too!)
- **Oasis (www.oasismag.com)** - This is an online-only publication created by and for gay and questioning youth.
- **POZ (www.poz.com)** - The focus of this magazine is HIV/AIDS and communicating the most up-to-date information about this disease to HIV+ people.
- **The Advocate (www.advocate.com)** - A newsmagazine for the gay and lesbian community.
- **XY (www.xymag.com)** - This is the most popular teen-oriented gay magazine in America. It combines hot (non-pornographic) pictures with excellent articles on a wide range of topics. It's a "must read" for gay teens!

Now, That's Entertainment!
Gay-Oriented Movie Suggestions: Take 1

■ **Broken Hearts Club** - Actors Dean Kane, Andrew Keegan, Kerr Smith and Michael Bergen, among others, play young (totally hot) gay characters in this dramatic comedy. (Rated R, Columbia TriStar Home Video, 2000, **www.thebrokenheartsclub.com**)

■ **Edge of Seventeen** - A gay teen finds out who he is and what he wants, who his friends are and who loves him, in this autobiographical tale set in the 1980s. (Not Rated, Strand Releasing, 1999)

■ **L.I.E.** - A 15-year-old Long Island boy loses everything and everyone he knows, then becomes involved in a relationship with an older man. (Rated NC-17, Lot 47 Films, 2001)

■ **Nico and Dani** - Two 17-year-old friends spend 10 days together on a summer holiday, and both learn about their emerging sexuality. Dani finds himself increasingly attracted to his friend Nico, whose interests lie only in losing his virginity before he goes home. Spanish with subtitles. (Not Rated, Avatar Films, 2001, **www.nicoanddani.com**)

■ **Adventures of Pricilla, Queen of the Desert** - Two drag queens and a transsexual get a cabaret gig in the middle of the desert. It's a classic! (Rated R, Gramercy Pictures, 1994)

■ **Trick -** This drama follows the adventures of two, young gay guys looking to be alone for a night in New York City. (Rated R, Fine Line Features, 1999)

■ **Queer As Folk** (Season One) - The entire first season of Showtime's awesome TV series is available on VHS and DVD. That's the first 22 American episodes featuring gorgeous actor Randy Harrison and the rest of the award-winning cast. (Rated R, Showtime Entertainment, 2001)

Chapter 2

Coming Out
Of The Closet

Until you confide in someone and reveal your sexual orientation to others, if you are, in fact, gay but hiding it, you're considered to be in the closet. With all of the pressures associated with being a gay teenager, there's nothing shameful about keeping your sexual orientation a secret from friends and family. Coming out of the closet takes a tremendous amount of courage. This chapter focuses on what it means to come out and what the possible positive *and* negative ramifications are.

Before you decide to come out and tell people you're gay, there are a handful of questions you should seriously consider. Some of these questions include:

- What does it mean to come out?
- Should I come out? If so, when?
- What's the best way to come out?
- Who should I come out to first?
- How might my life change once I come out to friends, family and/or everyone else?
- What happens if I get rejected by the people I'm close to, like family members or a best friend?
- What are the potential dangers of being an openly gay teenager?

Every single person on this planet, whether he's gay, bisexual or straight, has a different background and different life story. The way one person leads his or her life and the decisions he/she makes might be right for him/her, but 100 percent wrong for you. Thus, it's impossible to simply provide you with a list of steps to follow in order to answer the above questions that relate to coming out.

Everyone's situation is different. Thus, while this book and other people can provide you with advice and information about what others have experienced, only you can predict what the positive and/or negative consequences will be if and when you come out.

Your family upbringing and the open-mindedness of your parents, brothers, sisters and relatives; where you live; what the potential reaction of your close friends and the people at school will be; and what support resources you have available should all be carefully evaluated when you make the decision about whether or not to come out.

Of course, you can always come out only to your parents, only to one or more best friends, and/or to people you meet online, at clubs or at gay support groups, yet keep your sexual orientation a secret from everyone else. After all, your private life, your thoughts, feelings and sexual orientation are nobody's business but your own. You have the option to share this information with whomever you choose.

Keep in mind, by telling a few close friends, you always run the risk that your secret will be revealed to others. Once you confide in a friend, you have to trust him/her enough to keep your secret. Only you know how much you can trust your friends with highly personal information.

Since coming out can be a scary thing, many gay teenagers choose to open up first to people they meet online, at gay support groups or at clubs, or to a therapist or their doctor. Before coming out to your family and friends, it's important to first truly come to terms with the fact you're gay (or bisexual) and be somewhat comfortable with this.

Because coming out to your parents (and immediate family) can be an incredibly big deal, the next chapter is dedicated to this topic.

By first learning what it means to be gay through communication with other gay people, you'll obtain the knowledge and perhaps confidence you need. Interaction with other gay people will also help you begin to feel more comfortable about who you are. Creating a support system for yourself is important, not only for taking some of the stress out of the coming out process, but also to give you the moral support you'll need as you inform your parents, friends and/or those who are close to you.

Preparing to come out involves knowing how you'll react if someone you come out to doesn't take the information the way you expect them to. When you tell someone close to you you're gay, the emotions they'll experience may be unpredictable. Some people react with a sense of shock, anger or disbelief, or act as if they've been betrayed or lied to. Others are totally understanding and instantly supportive.

Assuming the person you tell doesn't react with strong negative emotions, anger and/or rejection, you can bet that upon coming out, you'll be asked a ton of questions. Be prepared to answer these questions as openly and honestly as possible. For example, if your best friend is a guy and he's straight, his first question might be, "Are you attracted to me?" Some of the questions you'll be asked may be stupid or funny, while others may seem harsh or downright mean, even though that wasn't the intent.

Keep in mind, people who are straight probably don't understand what it means to be gay. They've grown up learning all of the typical and inaccurate stereotypes.

Unfortunately, it becomes your job to set these people straight (no pun intended). When you come out to someone, the ultimate outcome will most likely be one of the following:

Scenario #1

- The person you confide in is understanding, loving and extremely supportive. He or she may or may not be totally shocked to learn you're gay. The person's response may be "No shit" or "I don't believe it." It all depends on how effeminate you are and how close you are to the people you tell. Some people may have suspected you were gay, but kept themselves in a state of denial. Some people's immediate reaction might be to apologize for any anti-gay comments they've ever made in front of you, then they start asking questions in hopes of better understanding what exactly it means that you're gay.

- The person you tell gets pissed off or feels betrayed. If the person doesn't know other people who are gay, they may experience a sense of confusion or feel extremely uncomfortable. Their instinct may be to distance themselves, either temporarily or permanently, from you. In these situations, unfortunately it becomes your responsibility to educate people who are misinformed or who don't understand what it means to be gay. While it may not be possible to communicate with people who distance themselves from you, ideally you want to make it clear that you are the same person you've always been. How individuals react to the news you're gay will be based a lot on their pre-existing misconceptions about homosexuals. You may find that after some time passes, once the person you come out to comes to terms with the news, they'll be more accepting than they were initially.

- The worst case scenario when you come out to someone close to you is that they'll react extremely negatively or perhaps violently. Coming out isn't something you want to rush into, before you're totally ready. Hopefully, when you do decide to come out, you'll initially select people you believe won't act this way. If you don't know how a particular person will react, chances are this isn't one of the first people you should come out to. If you suspect that someone might react violently or extremely negatively, it's an excellent idea to have someone else with you (such as a relative, friend or therapist you've already come out to).

Developing Your Support System

Throughout this book, the importance of developing a support system will be discussed repeatedly. Your support system could be comprised of one or more friends, family members, a therapist, other gay people (such as people you meet online or at support group meetings), or anyone else who is close to you. Those who make up your support system should be people you care about and trust. These are the people who will cheer you up when you're sad, offer you support when you're stressed out and provide you with the encouragement and love you need on a day-to-day basis.

The people in your support system will change as your life progresses. For example, as a small child, chances are it was your parents and/or grandparents who were included in your support system. As you've gotten older, you've probably begun to rely more on your best friends (classmates, teammates or fraternity brothers) for support, because these are the people who truly understand you and who you spend a lot of time with.

As you begin to explore your sexuality, the gay friends you meet, for example, may become a tremendous source of love and support. A therapist, guidance counselor or doctor whom you confide in as you explore your sexuality may also (for a time) be an integral part of your support system.

Photo (c) 2002 Mark V. Lynch, Latent Images

Ultimately, when you begin dating, your boyfriend will probably become an important part of your support system, as will your life partner (significant other or domestic partner) down the road. Because other gay people have had similar experiences to you, you'll find that the gay friends you make will share a non-sexual, but close bond with you that few straight people will be able to achieve. You'll eventually discover, if you haven't already, that the gay community as a whole, tends to be a close-knit community of people who often support one another.

When you begin to come out to the other people you're close to, such as your parents, relatives, straight friends, teammates, fraternity brothers, coworkers, peers, teachers, etc., the people in your support system will make the process much easier and less stressful, because you'll know you have people that love and support you, no matter how others react.

This additional support will provide you with a tremendous added level of confidence to face whatever trials and tribulations you may experience.

By developing a support system for yourself, even if it's comprised of only one person, you're less apt to feel alone, scared and depressed as you embark on life's journey.

If, at the moment, you're feeling totally isolated from the world and believe you have nobody to talk to, the best thing you can do for yourself is to make contact with other gay people online or attend a gay support group meeting. (For a list of local PFLAG chapters throughout the country, visit the group's Web site at **www.pflag.org**.) You can also call a support hotline if you need or want someone to talk to immediately.

Building a support system isn't as difficult as you might think. It does take a bit of work, but the love and care you'll receive is well worth the investment.

Coming Out:
Answers To Your Questions

Earlier in this chapter, several questions were posed. As you prepare to come out and reveal your sexual orientation to others, think carefully about these questions and the answers as they relate to your personal situation.

No matter what you read or what others tell you, only you can decide if coming out is the right thing for you to do. Likewise, it should be entirely your decision as to whom you come out to, when you break the news to others and how you tell them.

Are you absolutely sure about your sexual orientation? If not, you might want to refrain from coming out to friends and family. You may not be ready!

Coming out is a process. It's not just a matter of announcing to the world that you're gay. There are multiple steps involved with coming out. The order in which people experience these steps is different, based on their personal situations. The first step, however, is the same for everyone – you must admit the truth to yourself and accept it.

In addition to what you read here, also check out the following Web sites, which offer strategies for coming out, plus actual coming-out stories from young people.

www.EmptyClosets.com
www.ComingOutStories.com

After you come to terms with your own sexuality, the next logical step for many people is to meet and interact with other gay people (preferably around the same age as you). Chapters 4 and 7 offer a bunch of suggestions for meeting other gay people. It might be this group of people (or another gay individual) whom you'll come out to next. It's much easier to come out to someone else who is openly gay than it is to break the news to a straight person, especially a close friend or family member. An alternative to coming out first to another gay friend is to speak openly about your sexuality with a therapist, guidance counselor or your doctor, any of whom can offer you guidance and support.

Once you're sure of your sexual orientation and you're comfortable with it, you might choose to explore the possibility of sharing this information with those close to you. If you're not yet comfortable with being gay, even though you've come to terms with it, hold off telling friends and family until you're ready.

What Does It Mean To Come Out?

If you're keeping your sexual orientation a secret, you're still in the closet. Chances are, you've become used to acting straight and doing everything possible so that you're perceived as being straight by those around you. This becomes a habit and second nature to many people, especially those who keep their sexuality a secret for many years. It's pretty common for closeted gay teens to have girlfriends, just to keep up appearances.

Upon coming out, you no longer need to live a lie. There are no more secrets to keep and there is no longer a need to hide your sexual orientation – at least around the people you come out to.

For most people, coming out offers a tremendous relief and leads to a major life change. Even if you just confide in a best friend, your parents, a new friend who is gay or a therapist, for example, the sense of relief you'll feel will probably be tremendous.

At some point in your life (again for everyone the timing is different), you may reach a point when you don't care who knows about your sexuality. Thus, you can be openly gay. For some, this means wearing gay pride T-shirts, slapping a bumper sticker on their car and/or mounting a gay pride flag on their front door. For others, being openly gay means not caring if someone else finds out, but at the same time, not advertising it to the world.

Coming out means you're comfortable enough with yourself and your sexuality to share this information with at least one other person. Remember, who you tell, when you tell them and what details you choose to reveal are entirely up to you.

Should You Come Out? When?

The generic answer to this question is, yes, you should come out. However, everyone has a different situation, so coming out right now or in the immediate future might not be a good idea for you. This is a judgment call you need to make for yourself based on the information you gather, your comfort level and the support system you create for yourself.

Those who do choose to come out generally feel a tremendous sense of relief and increased self-esteem because the secret they've kept to themselves for so long is now out in the open (with at least one person).

Regarding when you should come out, this too depends on your personal situation. You may be ready to come out at age 12, or it might take you until age 35 to come to terms with your sexuality. When you do decide to share this information and have decided who you're going to confide in first, how you tell that person and the timing of your revelation is important. If the person you choose to tell is in the midst of his or her own life crisis, for example, the level of understanding and support you'll receive may be greatly diminished. Consider the other person's point of view and situation when choosing to come out.

The worst time to reveal your sexual orientation to someone is during an argument. Ideally, when you tell someone you're gay (or bisexual), you want it to be in a calm environment. Of course, you could always write a note or email, but the in-person approach typically works much better. Thus, try to avoid coming out to someone close to you (such as a best friend) over the telephone.

For people who are close to you, one of the worst ways they can learn about you being gay is from a third party or by accidentally catching you in a compromising situation with another guy. This creates a sense of tension and discomfort, which makes the coming-out process more complicated.

What's The Best Way To Come Out?

The best way for you to come out to others also varies greatly, based on who you're coming out to and what the situation is. Taking the direct, in-person approach in a calm and relaxed environment typically works best. Be prepared to have an open conversation with the person you're coming out to.

Consider these steps to assist in your preparation:

- Consider, in advance, what you want to say and how you want to say it.

- Choose the time and location carefully. Try to avoid loud and busy restaurants, where the people sitting next to you might listen in on the conversation.

- Think about the other person and what his/her needs are. Is the timing of your coming out okay for them? What else are they going through right now?

- During the coming-out process with each person you tell, make it clear that you're the same person you always have been and that nothing has changed.

- Be sure you're prepared to be open and honest with the person you're coming out to.

- Keep in mind, most people don't understand what being homosexual really means, so you'll probably need to explain the basics. For example, you'll probably need to explain that being gay isn't a decision you made, just as someone doesn't decide to be tall or short, left-handed or right-handed, or be born with brown eyes or blue eyes.

- Be prepared to receive a negative reaction from the person you're coming out to. Just as it might have taken you months or years to come to terms with your own sexuality, if the person you're telling is surprised, it could take him or her some time to adjust and accept the news. Try to keep the lines of communication open, but give the other person the time he or she needs to accept you as a gay person.

- Make sure you have your support system in place. This will be a tremendous comfort if things don't go as planned when you come out to others. Likewise, the people you come out to ultimately may need others they can talk to to deal with their feelings and concerns.

■ If you don't get the positive reaction you're hoping for when you come out, are you prepared to deal with the possible negative consequences, without taking the other person's reaction too personally? Being initially rejected by a close friend or relative can be emotionally devastating. It can also be a tremendous blow to your self-esteem if you're the type of person who needs the approval of others. If you get rejected by a person you come out to, it has to do with their own prejudices and misconceptions about homosexuals. It rarely, if ever, has anything to do with you. It's important you realize this. If after the initial shock wears off, the person you came out to isn't willing to work toward accepting you, the true nature of your relationship with the person (or the relationship you thought existed) should be reevaluated.

Who To Come Out To First?

In one word, this question can be answered. Okay, pop quiz! What's the answer? If you said, "Yourself," you're right! After accepting yourself and coming to terms with your own sexuality, you may choose to come out to any number of other people, such as:

■ A gay friend
■ A relative (such as an uncle or cousin)
■ Someone who you know is openly gay
■ Someone you've met online, at a gay club, at a gay support group meeting or by calling a toll-free hotline
■ Your best friend
■ Your brother(s) or sister(s)
■ Your fraternity brothers or teammates

- Your parents or grandparents (Be sure to read the next chapter for more information about coming out to your parents.)
- Your therapist, doctor or guidance counselor

Most gay people find it's much easier to come out first to someone outside of their immediate family.

Make sure, however, that the person you choose is open-minded and will be supportive. If you decide to confide in a teacher, for example, he or she is not obligated to keep your conversations confidential. A therapist, however, is required to keep quiet about whatever you discuss.

How Might Your Life Change Once You Become Openly Gay?

This too is a broad question with many possible answers, based on your own situation. While most people feel a sense of relief that they no longer need to live a lie and constantly act "straight," you do run the risk that other people will reject you because they have false impressions of what it means to be gay. As you already know, however, this is a reaction that's based upon incorrect stereotypes and misinformation.

Thanks in part to the growing popularity of gay characters and gay storylines on television shows and in movies, there's greater acceptance than ever among the general (straight) public. There are, however, people who hate gays, and who are very vocal about their feelings. Likewise, the statistics relating to gay hate-crimes involving teenagers are still high, so coming out to everyone and being openly gay could result in verbal or physical assault, depending on where you live and the people in your community. Not everyone experiences negative reactions, but unfortunately, if you choose to lead an openly gay life, it's something you may eventually have to deal with.

By first building up your support system, then selectively choosing who you come out to, the transition from being a closeted gay person to someone who has come out at least to friends and/or family (if not the entire world) can be a relatively smooth one.

The Human Rights Campaign offers a free downloadable brochure from its Web site, called *Resource Guide To Coming Out* (800-866-6263 / www.hrc.org). Within this brochure, Elizabeth Birch, executive director of The Human Rights Campaign wrote, "Let me assure you that being an openly gay, lesbian, bisexual or transgender person in this society is not always easy. But it is so much more gratifying than being in the closet. Hiding information and worrying that someone will discover your secret consumes a lot of personal energy. It also detracts from the quality of your life. No one should be denied the opportunity to thrive and flourish as a full human being because his or her sexual orientation or gender expression or identity is different from others."

What Happens If You Get Rejected By The People You're Close To?

Nobody likes rejection of any kind. It's important, however, that as you come out as a gay person in society, you accept that some people won't understand what being gay is all about. Hence, they won't understand you.

What's most important is that you surround yourself with caring, loving and supportive people. Hopefully, this includes your family members and current close friends. Once again, it's important to remember you're not alone. There are millions of other gay people in the world, and many of them could be your friend if you choose to open yourself up and become a part of the gay community.

If you do experience rejection from someone you truly care about, the best way to help the situation is to attempt to involve an intermediary, such as a therapist or another friend, who can intervene and help the other person come to terms with your sexual orientation and their feelings about it.

By seeking out a therapist, it doesn't necessarily mean you're in need of psychological help simply because you're gay. On the contrary! Meeting with a therapist isn't a weakness on your part. The sole purpose of the therapist might be to help you open a line of communication between you and a person you came out to who is having trouble accepting you.

> According to a 1994 statement made by the American Medical Association, "Most of the emotional disturbance experienced by gay men and lesbians around their sexual identity is not based on physiological causes, but rather is due more to a sense of alienation in an unaccepting environment."

If you're stuck, at least temporarily, in an unaccepting environment (at home, at school or at work, for example), seeking out emotional support is always a good idea.

While times are changing fast and people, especially other young people, are becoming more accepting of homosexuality, one study published by the *Journal of Sex Research* back in 1988 disclosed this rather upsetting statistic. "A national survey of heterosexual male youths 15 to 19 years of age found that only 12 percent felt that they could have a gay person as a friend. In a 14-city survey, nearly three-fourths of lesbian and gay youth first disclosed their sexual identity to friends. Forty-six percent lost a friend after coming out to her or him. In a study of gay and lesbian adolescents 14 to 21 years of age, less than one in five of the surveyed gay and lesbian adolescent students could identify someone who was very supportive of them."

Sure, even though it's outdated, reading a statistic like this is unsettling, especially if you're contemplating coming out to a friend. However, it's important to understand the potential upside *and* downside of coming out, before you actually make the decision.

Whether you're gay, bisexual or straight, it's important to lead the type of life you want to lead and that will insure your

Potential Risk – The Human Rights Watch released a figure indicating that each school year, two million adolescents are harassed physically or verbally for being – or appearing to be – gay, lesbian or bisexual.

happiness. Chances are, conforming to the expectations of others or succumbing to peer pressure to fit in won't make you happy. If you know you're gay, trying to be someone you're not in order to make other people happy probably isn't the best thing for you and certainly won't insure your happiness.

Are Your Friends True To You?

Friends are important to everyone, but true friends (the kind that will last a lifetime) will accept you for the person you are, whether you're straight, gay or bisexual. These are the types of friends you want. They're people you can rely on and trust. So-called friends who turn against you when they discover your true sexual orientation probably were never your friends at all.

Friendships that can withstand obstacles and pressures from the outside world are the ones truly worth maintaining. Remember, the more you put into a friendship, the more you'll get out of it. It's like any relationship.

Before coming out to a friend, ask yourself the following questions. Your answers to these questions will help you judge how receptive he or she will be when you tell'em you're gay.

- How has your friend reacted in the past, when the topic of homosexuality came up during conversations?
- Has your friend ever said anything positive or negative about homosexuality when seeing a gay person on the street, on television or in the movies?
- Does the person you're planning to come out to have other gay friends?
- How open-minded is your friend? What has he or she been taught or what's his or her perception of gay people?
- How much do you trust your friend?

What Are The Potential Dangers Involved with Being An Openly Gay Teenager?

Being openly gay is, of course, different from coming out to a few close friends and/or family members. If you're openly gay, and everyone in your community and your school knows it, there are potential dangers (and absolute worst-case scenarios).

For example, you could become an outcast at school or the victim of a hate crime. You might also be bullied for being gay. By coming out, if you think there's a real possibility of danger at this point in your life, keeping your sexuality a secret for now may be a good idea. Once you begin attending college, move away from home and/or have some more independence and control of your life, you can always readdress the situation.

Should you experience anything negative as a result of being gay or coming out, it's important that you don't face these challenges alone! It's perfectly acceptable to rely on your support team (family, friends and others) to offer you guidance and support during difficult phases of your life.

There are also numerous organizations that support gay teens who are victims of hate crimes and/or discrimination.

The following resources can also be used to help educate and enlighten people you choose to come out to:

■ The Lambda Legal Defense and Education Fund (**www.lambdalegal.org**) is a national organization committed to achieving full recognition of the civil rights of lesbians, gay men and people with HIV/AIDS through impact litigation, education and public policy work.

■ The National Youth Advocacy Coalition (**www.nyacyouth.org**), the only national organization solely focused on advocacy, education and information addressing the broad range of issues facing lesbian, gay, bisexual and transgender youth. The organization works to end discrimination against young people and to ensure their physical and emotional well-being. From the organization's Web site, you can download free copies of *Generation Out*, the coalition's quarterly newspaper.

■ SIECUS, the Sexuality Information and Education Council of the United States (**www.siecus.org**) is a national, nonprofit organization that asserts that sexuality is a natural and healthy part of living. Incorporated in 1964, SIECUS develops, collects and disseminates information, promotes comprehensive education about sexuality, and advocates the right of individuals to make responsible sexual choices.

If you choose to stay in the closet, make sure you're doing this for the right reasons. Are you simply making excuses and finding reasons not to come out as a result of being insecure? Being scared is normal. For most people, coming out is far less of a traumatic event than they anticipated, and once they open up about their sexual orientation with their friends and family, for example, they lead happier lives and are glad they made the decision to come out. Staying in the closet if you have a legitimate fear is one thing, but making countless excuses due to personal insecurities and self-doubt is something you can and should try to overcome.

Photo (c) 2002 Mark V. Lynch, Latent Images

Chapter 3

Coming Out
To Your Parents

Shout Out America
Q: Who did you come out to first?
How did you do it?

"Right before my 17th birthday, I came out to my mom. After talking with some friends about what to do, I told her I needed to talk to her. I don't think I needed to actually say anything. She knew what was coming."
- Josh, 18, Atlanta, GA

"My mom. I purposely left a copy of *XY* magazine out when I went on a weekend trip. When I came home, I told her I had kissed a boy. She said she found the magazine and already knew. We both cried. I was 16 at the time."
- Tristan, 19, Los Angeles, CA

"When I was 14, I told a close female friend over the telephone that I liked guys. I said I was bisexual, because that seemed easier. Two months into my 9th grade year, I came out to everyone, one person at a time, and asked them not to tell others." - Michael, 21, Ft. Lauderdale, FL

"I came out on Valentine's Day 2002. I told my friends first. Their response was, 'Seriously, are you?' After I told them, my friends had a much higher level of respect for me. I'm currently dating one of my friends. I knew I was gay for about four years before I told anyone."
- Luke, 18, Erie, PA

"I've known I was gay for as long as I can remember. It was just a feeling I've always had. I finally came out when I was 17. The first person I told was my older sister. I then told a few close friends. Later, I told my mom. Most recently, I came out to my dad and older brother. It could not have gone better. Nobody's feelings changed toward me. If anything, it's brought me closer to the people I've come out to."
- Kyle, 18, Boulder, CO

As a gay teenager, one of the scariest and potentially hardest things you'll experience is the prospect of coming out to your parents and family members. There are no easy answers or solutions for dealing with this, nor are there any guaranteed ways to insure your parents will deal with learning that you're gay in a positive manner.

If you come out to your friends and they reject you, you can always make new friends. If, however, your parents and/or relatives reject you, that's much harder to deal with, especially if you're financially dependant on your parents and still living with them. Whatever the case, chances are, when you come out to your parents, the relationship you share with them will change, hopefully for the better, but possibly for the worse (at least temporarily).

Should You Come Out To Your Parents?

Only you can answer this question, but there are some extremely good reasons why you might want to consider coming out. Here's what the folks at PFLAG have to say:

> *"Coming out is a way for gay, lesbian, bisexual and transgendered people to live their lives openly and honestly. People come out because staying 'in the closet' keeps the important people in their lives from knowing about a big part of their identity. Hiding one's sexual orientation or gender identity can be very stressful, lonely and isolating. Many gay people fear rejection from their families, friends, co-workers and religious institutions. However, in most cases, the stress of keeping a secret from the people they are close to ultimately outweighs the fear of losing acceptance and love. Coming out is an im-*

portant decision that people should be able to make on their own terms - when they want to, to whom they want to. Fear, misinformation, stereotypes and societal prejudice, can make coming out a very difficult process for both gay people and for the friends and family they come out to. PFLAG can help [with this process]."

For all teenagers (gay or straight), there is almost always going to be some tension, at least periodically, between you and your parents as you become more independent, have more freedom and become more mature. People have different relationships with their parents, yet if you're contemplating coming out to them, chances are you're in for some emotional, confusing and possibly difficult times ahead.

Even if your parents are the most open-minded, loving and supportive people on the planet, few parents want their son to be gay. After all, when most parents hear this news, their immediate (albiet selfish) reaction is that their hopes and dreams for you have been shattered.

Some parents focus on their incorrect stereotypes of gay people and immediately think they'll never have grandchildren, that you're destined to have a life filled with misery and that you'll probably die young from AIDS. Based on the religious upbringing and faith of your parents, a whole set of other questions and concerns may also come into play.

Virtually all parents experience a sense of grief upon hearing their son is gay, mainly because they believe they've failed.

Your sexual orientation somehow becomes entirely their fault. They feel ashamed, guilty and angry, and these feelings could be taken out on you in a variety of ways. The initial reaction of your parents might also be that they fear what other relatives or neighbors will think, especially if homosexuality is frowned upon in your family or community.

Even if you've come to terms with your own sexuality, coming out to your parents at this point in your life may or may not be a good idea, based on your relationship with them and how you believe they'll respond to the news. By exposing your secret, do you run the risk of being disowned, thrown out of the house, being cut off financially, getting beaten or somehow emotionally abused?

When you come out to your parents, they'll typically experience several strong emotions in the hours, days, weeks and months that follow. These emotions will be experienced in stages, and will most likely include: shock, denial, guilt, an expression of feelings, personal decision-making and hopefully true acceptance.

In some situations, upon learning their son is gay, parents panic and don't know how to react, or they react rashly by forcing their child to see a psychiatrist, doctor or priest, for example. Working under the misconception that being gay is a disease that can be cured, parents might unfortunately take actions that are not necessarily in your best interest.

If your parents insist you seek professional help, here are some suggestions from PFLAG about how to deal with this situation:

1) You might be ready to suggest the name of a counselor or two [for your parents] if your parents think that counseling will help to clarify their confusion. It would be advisable to suggest a

non-gay person, because your parents will want an "unbiased" view.

2) If they press for you to see a counselor, suggest that they match you session-for-session. They may resist on the grounds that they don't need help; underneath, however, they'll probably welcome someone to talk to.

While you may want and need support from your parents, chances are, you'll be the one needing to provide support for them. For example, you may need to assure them that your sexual orientation has no relevance to their parenting or how you were brought up. You may or may not consider your mother and father to be good parents for a multitude of reasons. However, there is no scientific evidence to support the idea that the way a child is brought up can lead to homosexuality.

Nobody deserves to be mistreated physically or mentally because of their sexuality. If you're gay or bisexual, there's nothing abnormal about you, and you should never be convinced that your sexual orientation somehow makes you less of a person. Should you decide to come out to your parents, it's critical that you have a support system in place and have other people you can rely on for moral support.

> Before coming out to your parents, it becomes your responsibility to obtain a comfort level with yourself, so you'll be able to educate your parents in order to counteract whatever misconceptions they may have about homosexuality.

Based on your own situation and the relationship you have with your parents, it may be an excellent idea to bring in a third person, such as another relative (whom you've already come out to), a close friend, a guidance counselor or a therapist, to help you come out to your parents and help your parents deal with their own reactions.

There are plenty of books and resources specifically designed to help parents deal with their emotions and concerns once they learn their child is gay. By directing your parents to these resources, their acceptance of the news about your sexual orientation could happen faster. For example, you might consider bringing one or both of your parents to a PFLAG meeting in your city.

As difficult as it may be for you to come to terms with your sexuality and then choose to reveal this information to your parents, almost every parent will have an equally difficult time accepting this information, whether or not they show it.

Just as it's taken you months or perhaps years to accept yourself, if the news that you're gay comes as an absolute shock to your parents, they might not come to terms with the news immediately, so try to be patient and understanding.

On the other hand, your mom and/or dad may have suspected you were gay for a while now and have had time to come to terms with it, but they were too scared to ask you. By coming out, you may immediately build a closer and stronger bond with your parents. Again, everyone's situation is different.

Ask Yourself These Questions

Before coming out to your parents, take time to think and plan. Also, ask yourself these questions, and be totally honest with yourself as you contemplate the answers. These questions will help you predict what might happen when you come out to your parents.

- Are you totally sure you're gay (or bisexual)? If you're not sure, it might not be the right time to come out. When you tell your parents, some of their first questions will most likely be, "Are you sure?," "Could this just be a phase?" or "How long have you known?"

- Have you come to terms with your sexual orientation? Do you fully understand that being gay is not your choice and that it's perfectly normal?

- How do you think your parents will react to the news?

- Do you think your parents already know (or suspect) you're gay, but have been too scared to ask you?

- Once you reveal you're gay to your parents, what's the best possible reaction you hope to receive (based on how well you know them)? What can you do to help insure you'll receive this reaction?

- Considering how well you know your parents, what's the absolute worst case scenario that could happen if you come out to them? Are you prepared to face and are you capable of dealing with whatever happens? Are you prepared to wait a week, six months or even a few years for them to fully come to terms with your homosexuality? What happens if you get cut off financially and/or thrown out of your house?

- Do you have a support team in place to provide you with the emotional support you'll need?

- Can you help your parents better understand homosexuality?

- If you think now is the right time to come out, what's your personal motivation? According to PFLAG, "Hopefully, you're coming out because you love them [your parents] and are uncomfortable with the distance you feel. Never come out in anger or during an argument, using your sexuality as a weapon."

- Do you have any gay relatives? Do your parents have gay friends? How comfortable are your parents around other gay people?

- What is the moral or religious view your parents have about homosexuality in general? Have they been brought up thinking being gay is wrong? What are the religious implications?

- Is there someone you'd like to have with you when you come out to your parents?

- Do you think it's best to come out first to either your mother or father, before revealing your sexual orientation to both parents at once? Is one of your parents more apt to be understanding and supportive?

- Based on everything that's going on in your parent's lives (with their jobs, family life, etc.), is the timing right to come out to your parents?

- If you do decide to come out, what's the best approach to take that will make the event as easy as possible for both you and your parents? Choose the best time and location. It's also an excellent idea to plan out exactly what you'll say and how you'll say it. While you could always come out by writing a letter, you'll be better able to immediately deal with your parent's positive (or negative) reactions if you come out to them in person.

Dealing With One Parent At A Time

If you decide to tell only one parent and want that parent to keep your secret from their husband or wife, you may be asking a lot. In all fairness, make sure the parent you decide to tell has someone he/she can talk to and confide in (such as another relative, a friend or a therapist), in order to help them deal with their own emotions and concerns. Remember, coming out to your parents doesn't mean you're required to reveal your sexual orientation to other relatives, such as your grandparents, sister(s), brother(s), aunt(s) or uncle(s). This may or may not be something you choose to do now or down the road.

Yes, there's a lot to consider before coming out to your parents. After all, you're trusting them enough to reveal something very personal about yourself (a secret you might have been holding inside for years) – something they might not be too happy about or comfortable with.

First Things First

When and if you decide to come out, try to anticipate all of the questions, thoughts and concerns your parents will have and be ready to address everything head-on, when you actually come out. It's up to you to choose the best way to tell your parents.

Think carefully about what you'll say, how you'll say it and when the best time to come out is. Develop a plan, and if necessary, write the plan down. It's okay to write down exactly what you want to say. Chances are, when you actually sit down to talk with your parents, you're going to be nervous. Having notes may help keep you from forgetting anything.

During the coming out process, be prepared to convince your parents that your sexual orientation isn't their fault, if you're sexually active you know the dangers of HIV/AIDS, you're the same person you've always been, and nothing anyone can do will change your sexual orientation.

Also, make it clear you still love your parents dearly (if this is the case), and that you don't blame your homosexuality on them – it is nobody's fault, nor it is a decision you've made or a disease you've caught. Your sexual orientation isn't a preference.

When, If Ever, Should You Come Out To Your Parents?

Whether or not you decide to come out to your parents (and when) is up to you. This should not be something you're forced or guilted into doing by anyone. At the same time, however, think about what would happen if your parents accidentally find out from someone else. What if you get caught in a compromising situation with another guy or your parents intercept a personal email message?

It's true, some people never come out to their parents. Others wait until they've graduated from high school or college, have moved out of their parents' home and are financially self-sufficient. There are also gay teenagers, however, who feel totally comfortable revealing their sexual orientation to their parents at a young age, and upon doing so, experience little or no negative repercussions. In fact, their relationship with their parents gets better.

As someone who is gay and thinking about whether or not to come out to your parents, you have the following options. Which of these options you choose should be based on your relationship with your parents and your own comfort level.

When To Come Out To Your Parents: The Options

- You come out to your parents as soon as you yourself come to terms with the fact that you're gay.

- You wait to come out until you're in your first serious relationship with another guy.

- You wait to come out to your parents until you've graduated from school, have moved out of your house and you're financially self-sufficient.

- You stay in the closet forever (in terms of your parents), never revealing your sexual orientation to them.

Take Things Slowly!

Ultimately, most parents come to terms with the fact they have a gay son and life goes on. Assuming you receive full acceptance, love and support from your parents, don't overwhelm them. For example, a week after coming out, don't start inviting your boyfriend to spend the night (if you still live with your parents).

If you have a serious boyfriend, perhaps it would be beneficial to give your parents a chance to meet and get to know him. (Again, a lot has to do with your personal situation and your relationship with your parents and your boyfriend.) If your parents see how happy you are and they like the guy you're dating, they're more apt to be accepting. Seeing you with a guy and knowing he's your boyfriend may be a bit overwhelming for your parents at first, so for a while, it might be a good idea to refrain from kissing or being overly affectionate in front of your parents.

Instead of taking an "in your face" approach with your parents, be open and honest if you decide to come out, then allow things to happen naturally. While you must focus on your own happiness and well-being, there's no need to be selfish and make things harder for your parents on purpose, even if you don't feel you're receiving the acceptance, love and support you need from them.

Finally, keep in mind that it's common for one parent to be more understanding or more readily accepting of your sexuality than the other. After all, each of your parents had a different upbringing and has his or her own thoughts and beliefs about homosexuality. You may need to deal with each of your parents separately as you come out to them. Also, don't be surprised if their initial reaction puts some stress on their relationship with each other, especially if they have opposing viewpoints. Try to keep all lines of communication open with both of your parents.

While this book can't tell you to come out to your parents, or recommend that you stay in the closet, hopefully it is providing you with enough background information to make intelligent and well-thought-out decisions for yourself.

The best strategy is always to hope for the best, but prepare in advance for the worst when coming out to your parents and other close relatives. For many, getting this secret off their chest relieves a tremendous emotional burden.

> If, after reading this book, you're still unsure about how to proceed, don't be afraid to seek out the support and guidance of other gay people or accept assistance from a support group (such as PFLAG or a Gay/Straight Alliance at your school).

Resources Are Available

For help coming up with and evaluating your answers to the questions posed in this chapter, you can download a free brochure entitled '*Coming Out To Your Parents*' from the PFLAG Web site (**www.pflagphila.org/brochure.htm**).

To help your parents deal with their emotions and feelings, you might download the '*Out Proud: Be Yourself – For Parents of Gay Children*' (**www.outproud.org/ brochure_for_parents.html**) brochure, print it out, then give it to your parents when you actually come out.

Using any Internet search engine, such as Yahoo! or Google, use the search phrase "Coming Out To Parents" in order to find the vast amount of information that's available online. You'll also find many books (in bookstores, libraries and online) that cover this topic.

Most importantly, to help you prepare to come out to your parents, talk with a handful of other gay people who have already come out and learn from their experiences. Determine what their experiences were really like, what challenges they faced and what they did to achieve success in revealing their sexual orientation to their parents.

Shout Out America

Q: What were your parents' reactions when you came out? Has anything changed since?

"First, I told my sister, when I was 22. I explained that the kid I was always hanging out with was my boyfriend. I came out to my parents a short time later when they asked me. At first, they cried. They still don't like it, but they're trying to accept it. They still don't want to see me and my boyfriend holding hands or openly showing affection."

- Eric, 25, Boston, MA

"I am extremely happy I came out to my parents! Their initial reaction was they cried. Now, they've come to terms with it and love it. We were driving in the car together and it popped out. I was 14 at the time."
- Richard, 16, Pinellas Park, FL

I haven't come out to my parents. I'm going to wait until I move out of the house. I came out to my friends when I was 20. All of my friends were very positive and supportive. Some said they already knew. Since then, that aspect of my life has gotten better, because I can be me. I don't have to feel like an outsider."
- Joe, 21, Minneapolis, MN

"I came out in my senior year of high school. My parents are pretty open-minded, so it didn't seem to bother them. They just want me to be happy and safe. My mom had several openly gay friends. She sort of already knew I was gay. They experienced neither shock or disgust when I told them. I think it brought us all closer together."
- Jared, 21, Miami, FL

Chapter 4

The Gay
Social Scene

By now, hopefully you realize that just because you're gay you're not alone in the world. There are plenty of other gay people in the same situation as you, plus countless others who are currently leading happy and productive lives.

While the next chapter focuses more on dating and the romantic aspects of gay life, this chapter focuses on ways to expand your circle of friends to include other gay people. Having straight friends is important, as is maintaining the closest possible relationship with your family, but for someone who is gay, finding other gay people to hang out with, confide in and share your experiences with can be an awesome experience.

Should you give up all of your straight friends now that you know you're gay? No way! Just because you're gay, you don't automatically become an outcast in straight society. For many, maintaining or developing close friendships with straight people is a perfectly normal thing.

The key to happiness is to surround yourself with people you truly care about – whether they're gay, straight or bisexual, males or females. Love, trust, honesty, acceptance, shared interests and the willingness to support one another are the key ingredients for any good friendship.

How do you like to spend your free time? No matter what you enjoy doing, whether it's watching or participating in sports, going to movies or shopping, for example, chances are, these activities are a lot more fun if you have friends to do them with.

Obviously, not everyone you spend your time with is going to become your best friend. If there's a straight person from work you enjoy spending your breaks with, or a friend from the gym who makes working out more entertaining, that's great. As you go through life, you'll meet many people. Some will become close friends, while many may remain casual acquaintances or come and go from your life.

Ideally, you want to surround yourself with people who bring out the best in you and who encourage you to be your best, at whatever it is you set out to do. Your friends and the people you spend time with should be a source of encouragement, inspiration and support. Remember, a friendship is all about give and take. If you want to develop close friendships, you have to be a good friend in return. Likewise, it's not necessary to become a groupie or conformist, just to fit in. Be yourself and find people to spend your time with who accept and respect you for the person you are. Many potential friends and acquaintances are out there – you just need to find them!

While plenty of gay people enjoy perfectly normal lives living, going to school and working among straight people, many find it reassuring or just fun to hang out or interact with other gay people. Whatever your personal situation is, if you decide to become part of the gay community, there are good friends to be made and fun times to be had.

Defining Your Image

Many gay teens are forced to lead two distinct lives. At school and perhaps at home as well, you're forced to stay in the closet, act "straight" and do whatever is necessary to fit in. At the same time, if there is an openly gay aspect of your life, at the clubs or online, for example, you're free to express yourself and convey whatever image you choose.

Gay people come in all shapes and sizes. Some are tall, short, fat, skinny, muscular, light skinned, dark skinned, etc. While there are stereotypical categories a gay person may fit into, like being a jock, muscle stud or a twink, there's no reason why you need to fit into any category.

Whether you're gay, bisexual or straight, be yourself, especially when it comes to your appearance. What you wear, how you style your hair, the jewelry you wear, how you carry yourself and the ways you express yourself through body language

What's a 'twink?' It's a slang term for a cute, young, toned, but not too intelligent gay guy. It's like when a girl is called a 'chick.'

all help to create your overall image and determine how others will perceive you.

Your personal tastes typically impact your appearance. After all, you choose the clothing you wear and how your hair gets styled. Everyone has their own style. It's part of what makes us all individuals. While some of us attempt to fit in by adjusting our personal style to be compatible with a group of people, others are more comfortable expressing their own individuality.

As you attempt to define your image, whether you're acting straight or don't care if your appearance somehow celebrates your gayness, do what feels comfortable. Try borrowing ideas from magazines, your peers, your favorite TV shows and what the hottest stars are wearing, then try out the ideas on yourself to see what looks good and what works for you. Of course, you can also go shopping with friends and ask for their opinions.

Ultimately, the image you create for yourself should be one you truly like. If you're happy with your appearance, you'll be more confident in everything you do, including making new friends and socializing.

Remember, nobody is perfect! Everybody has something about their appearance they'd like to change or improve upon. However, now is not the time to be thinking about plastic surgery or taking drastic steps to alter your appearance.

Photo (c) 2002 Mark V. Lynch, Latent Images

Just because you're gay, you don't have to transform yourself into a muscle stud or one of those pretty boys you see modeling in magazines. Those are images of near perfection that few people can live up to. Focus on being yourself, and be proud of who you are, physically and emotionally.

As a teenager, focus on your health. Take care of yourself by eating right, getting enough sleep and exercising, for example. You can always supplement these activities by adopting a skin care regime to maintain a clear complexion, using styling products on your hair, whitening your teeth (with specialized products and/or toothpaste) and wearing various fashions that accent your best physical assets. By coming to terms with the person you are and accepting it, you'll quickly discover the people around you will accept you as well.

Maintaining Your Good Complexion

There are many over-the-counter products designed to help you develop and maintain a clear complexion. Keeping your skin clean and healthy looking will improve your overall image and confidence. If you're concerned about your complexion, consult a doctor or dermatologist.

If you're interested in an easy-to-follow, three-step skin care regime, visit any major department store and take a look at the Clinique Skin Supplies For Men (**www.clinique.com**) product line. The three step process involves: **cleaning** (to remove accumulated oil and dirt), **exfoliating** (to sweep away dead flakes that dull your skin's appearance and clog pores) and **moisturizing** (to keep your skin smooth and soft).

While the Clinique product line is a bit pricey, there are many less expensive products and skin care regimens you can use to clean, exfoliate and moisturize your skin to maintain a clear and healthy-looking complexion.

Your Straight Friends

Obviously, you don't want to hang around people who are prejudiced or homophobic toward you. As a gay teenager and someone who has perhaps been verbally or physically abused by straight people because of your sexuality, it's important for you to be able to coexist in the straight world. After all, even if you live a gay life, chances are, as you get older, you'll still need to attend high school and/or college, then work and live among straight people – and hopefully fit in.

As a gay teenager, your middle school and high school years will probably be your hardest in terms of the cruelty you experience from your peers. Young people can be mean! They tease anyone who doesn't fit into the norm. Thus, if you're short, fat, tall, skinny, an ethnic minority, wear glasses, possess some type of disability or you're gay, chances are you're going to be teased in school. Unfortunately, it's part of life and it sucks, especially if you're on the receiving end of being teased, bullied or harassed. Never take this treatment personally. Often, the bullies are lashing out at someone perceived to be weaker because for some reason their own lives suck.

The good news is, people grow up a lot in their late-teens and early twenties. By the time you reach college age, chances are, you'll find people who are a lot more accepting of you and who you are. Try to be patient and confident. If the social aspect of your life is awful right now, things will improve in the future.

Developing a circle of straight friends as well as gay friends will help you lead a normal, well adjusted and well balanced life. Being gay is a sexual orientation. It's not necessarily a defining factor for who you are as a person or something that needs to impact every other aspect of your life. You can have a meaningful romantic relationship with a guy, but otherwise lead a perfectly normal life (by choice) at school, at work and in your day-to-day life.

Ideally, if you have straight friends, they should be people who know you're gay. Otherwise, you're keeping a huge part of your life a secret from them. However, at this point in your life, staying closeted may be important to you. While your gay friends will help you feel more comfortable in terms of your sexual orientation, straight friends can help you exist happily in the everyday world and be accepted in that world.

Someone's sexual orientation should not be a deciding factor when it comes to your friendships, no more than someone's gender, skin color or ethnic background should be. If you're still in school, making straight friends will probably be a lot easier than making gay friends, since it'll be the straight people you're pretty much surrounded by.

Making Gay Friends

No matter how conservative or homophobic your town, city or community may be, one thing is for certain – you're not the only gay person living there. While you may not see guys walking down the streets holding hands, like you would in West Hollywood, California or Provincetown, Massachusetts, for example, there are other gay people who live, go to school and/ or work near you. That's a fact!

The trick to meeting other gay people is first to discover where they hang out. This section will give you some ideas about how and where to meet other gay guys in your area. Of course, one of the easiest and best ways to become a voice in the gay community, without ever leaving your home or dorm room, is to get yourself online and check out the gay-oriented chat rooms, for example.

Be sure to check out Chapter 6 to discover some of the best places to meet gay guys online. If you're looking to take the in-person approach to meeting people, this chapter will be useful.

So, the big question is, where do gay dudes (who are openly gay or still in the closet) hang out? While every community, town and city is different, the following are a few ideas for places worth checking out.

Before seeking out new gay friends, ask yourself what you're looking for. Out of the following suggestions for places to meet other gay guys, some are more appropriate than others, based on what you're looking to get out of the experience.

If you're looking for friends around your own age (who happen to be gay), attending a gay support group meeting or visiting the mall, for example, might provide what you're looking for. If you're looking to hook up, a gay bar might be more appropriate (assuming you're of legal age).

Pay Attention To Your Gaydar!

Keep in mind, unless you're at an all-gay event or a gay club, for example, not every cute guy you run into is going to be gay (bummer, huh?). Chances are, you already have "gaydar", which is a natural ability to pick out other gay people in an otherwise straight crowd. Gaydar (which some say stands for GAY Detection And Ranging) is kind of like ESP or an intuitive "sixth sense" among gay people.

As you become part of the whole gay social scene, your gaydar will become more reliable, whether or not you believe it's an actual psychic ability. It's something that'll evolve naturally. When you think someone might be gay, try making eye contact and offer a friendly smile. At first, any communication you'll have will be an unspoken thing. If there's prolonged (and mutual) eye contact and perhaps you receive a flirtatious smile back, then you can be more secure in walking up and starting a conversation. Never simply assume someone else is gay unless you're in a totally gay-oriented environment. Also, even if you're a total believer in gaydar, it's never 100 percent accurate. So, trust your instincts, but proceed with caution.

Illegal Drug Use Among Gay Teens

The truth is, life isn't always perfect for gay, bisexual or questioning teens. How you deal with the trials and tribulations of life, however, can have a lasting impact on the rest of your life. Remember, you control your actions and can make your own decisions!

Too many young people, starting as early as age 12 (according to statistics), turn to drug use and alcohol as a way to escape from their everyday problems. In fact, in the next 24 hours, over 15,000 teenagers will experiment with drugs for the first time. You don't have to become a statistic.

With drugs and alcohol being so prevalent in the gay social scene (at clubs and parties, for example), you will probably be offered these substances. Like straight teens, you'll also be exposed to peer pressure and encouraged to experiment. You might be told, "Everyone is doing it," "Try it once, it won't hurt you" or "Loosen up, it's fun!"

The truth is, while the short-term effect of drugs or alcohol may be pleasurable, the impact these substances have on your body in the long-term isn't good. In many instances, an addiction can easily and quickly be developed, causing your life to spin out of control even more, before you realize what's happening. In addition, there are many dangers involved with mixing various drugs with alcohol, and you can accidently overdose on a drug.

When you're using any type of drugs or alcohol, your ability to think clearly and your judgement becomes greatly impaired. Your memory is also impacted. Thus, you're more apt to get yourself into a dangerous situation, either with someone who wants to take advantage of you or while driving, for example. A huge percentage of gay rapes happen when the victim is drunk or under the influence of drugs.

There's a big difference between 'experimenting' and becoming a regular user of illegal drugs or alcohol. If you find yourself getting out of control, seek help.

Teen Help (**800-840-5704 / www.vpp.com/teenhelp**) is a free resource that provides referrals and support. MADD (Mothers Against Drunk Driving, **www.madd.org**) and SADD (Students Against Destructive Decisions, **www.saddonline.com**) are two national organizations with local chapters in communities and cities throughout America. Both offer information and support for teenagers who abuse drugs and/or alcohol.

Everyone has problems they'd like to forget about and escape from. It's also normal to want to have fun at parties or when clubbing. The decisions you make about drug and alcohol usage, however, will have lasting implications for your life, plus could negatively impact the lives of those around you.

According to the U.S. Department of Health and Human Services, "Heroin, cocaine, and alcohol in combination with other drugs were the three most common substances in drug-related deaths reported by medical examiners participating in the Drug Abuse Warning Network (DAWN) in 2000. Narcotic analgesics - including methadone, codeine, hydrocodone and oxycodone - also frequently ranked in the top 10 drugs mentioned by medical examiners in the DAWN mortality report."

Common Drugs

Depending on the drug, it can be ingested, injected, smoked and/or inhaled (snorted). However it gets into your system, you can bet that the pleasurable effects won't last long. Before you know it, you'll be experiencing your everyday life once again, and you'll also have to deal with the negative and often lasting impact the drugs have on your mind and body. Thus, whatever problems you thought you had before drinking or taking drugs, will most likely be worse after the pleasurable effects of the drugs wear off.

At the clubs and at parties, in addition to alcohol, some of the more common drugs include: Ectasy, cocaine, speed, LSD, GHB, Chrystal meth (a pure form of speed) and Ketamine. Each has its own impact on your mind and body, based on how it's taken. Some of these drugs dramatically increase the chances of a stroke among young people.

One drug to watch out for is Rohypnol, which is known as the 'date rape drug' or 'roofies.' It is a brand name for flunitrazepam (a benzodiazepine), a very potent tranquilizer similar in nature to valium (diazepam), but many times stronger. The drug produces a sedative effect, amnesia, muscle relaxation and a slowing of psychomotor responses. Sedation occurs 20 to 30 minutes after administration and lasts for several hours. The drug is often distributed on the street in it's original "bubble packaging" which adds an air of legitimacy and makes it appear to be legal.

Rohypnol can be mixed with alcohol or other drugs to create a very fast-acting and powerful high. It also lowers inhibitions. This combination makes it a perfect tool for sexual predators to use on unsuspecting or naive teen guys at clubs or parties.

Places To Meet Gay People

Are you ready to meet other gay dudes in person? The following (listed in alphabetical order) are some suggestions as to where other gay guys might be hanging out in your area:

Bathhouses

A bathhouse or gay sex club should not be your first choice as a place to meet other gay guys! Saunas, hot tubs, swimming pools, locker rooms, communal showers, private cabanas (containing TVs and VCRs playing gay porn) plus common areas are typically what make up a gay bathhouse. Why do people visit these places? Typically, it's to meet other guys, show off their naked bodies and ultimately hook up.

There's a huge portion of the gay population that wouldn't be caught dead visiting a gay bathhouse. Due to the negative reputation these places developed as HIV/AIDS began to spread in the gay community, there aren't too many gay bathhouses left, but in some cities they still exist.

If you choose to visit one of these places and participate in the activities, don't be stupid! Use protection and proceed with caution! If you're under age, don't even bother.

Digital City: The Gay Local Scene (www.DigitalCity.com or AOL Keyword: **Gay Local Scene**) allows you to check out what's happening in any major U.S. city (or region) in terms of the gay-oriented clubs, local events, parades, festivals, theater, etc. This is a great resource to learn what's happening in your area, or to help you discover what's going on in cities you'll be traveling to.

Bookstores

For some reason, those book superstores that have been popping up across America have become a popular gay hangout. Many gay guys (and straight people, for that matter) enjoy hanging out on the couches, drinking gourmet coffee, reading books and socializing. This certainly isn't the case at all large bookstores, so see what the local vibe is in your community.

Typically, in the bookstores where gay people do hang out, the environment is extremely casual and safe. It's relatively easy to strike up conversations and make introductions.

If there's a gay bookstore in your community, you can pretty much bet that the people who frequent the store are gay.

Cafés / Coffee Houses

In some areas, cafés and coffee houses are frequented by the local gay population. These places offer a place for gay friends to meet, kick back, dine and socialize in a casual environment. In gay-oriented locales, like West Hollywood, California; Provincetown, Massachusetts; Ft. Lauderdale, Florida or Key West, Florida; for example, cafés and coffee houses typically attract an upscale and sophisticated gay crowd, made up of people of all ages.

If you're in the West Hollywood area, during the day, The Abbey (692 North Robertson, **310-855-9977, www.abbeyfoodandbar.com**), for example, is a low-key café for gay people of all ages to relax, eat and socialize. At night, The Abbey becomes one of West Hollywood's premier gay hotspots.

College

On many college campuses, you'll find a student-run gay and lesbian organization. Some of these groups are open to the general public (not just enrolled students). Participating in one of these groups is an excellent way to meet gay men in their late-teens and early-twenties, in a highly social and open environment.

Many colleges and universities welcome qualified students, no matter what their sexual orientation happens to be. As you're applying to schools, consider investigating whether or not the school offers organized programs for its gay students. Also, be sure to look into financial aid programs and scholarships specifically for gay and bisexual guys.

For information about some of the financial aid and scholarship programs specifically for gay and bisexual men, point your Web browser to one of the following sites:

- **www.finaid.org/otheraid/gay.phtml**
- **www.realcollegelife.com/pre-college/scholar-ships/gay-les.htm**

Gay Friendly Colleges

As you explore and research different colleges, determine what each school you're interested in offers in terms of its official policy on sexual orientation. Ask if the school's 'Equal Opportunity Policy Statement' actually mentions sexual orientation.

Does the school promote a public policy that prohibits discrimination based on sexual orientation? You may find this information in the school's admissions catalog or literature. However, you can also contact the school's admissions department directly.

In addition to an official policy, try to determine how active the gay and lesbian community is on campus. How large is the membership? Are faculty members involved? Is the organization funded by the school? Does the group sponsor organized events? Whether or not you choose to be vocal about your sexuality and active with the group once you're attending the school is your decision. For now, use the group as a gauge for determining how welcome you'll be as a gay or bisexual student.

To help you find gay friendly colleges, check out the various college directories at bookstores and at the college placement office of your high school. One excellent directory is *Best 331 Colleges*, published by Princeton Review (**www.review.com**).

The Princeton Review survey of 65,000 students at 331 colleges is the largest on-going poll of student opinions about their colleges. At each college, a random sample of students (200 per campus on average) answers 70 questions about their own school's academics, campus life and student body, as well as their study hours, politics and opinions.

While the following is based on a single survey, *Best 331 Colleges* (2002 Edition) reports the following 20 colleges and universities as having received the highest ranks in terms of being gay friendly:

1. Smith College
2. New York University
3. Drew University
4. Wesleyan University
5. Colby College
6. Simon's Rock College of Bard
7. Connecticut College
8. Pitzer College
9. Reed College

10. Vassar College
11. Sarah Lawrence College
12. Wells College
13. Boston University
14. Barnard College
15. Whitman College
16. University of California – Berkeley
17. Lewis & Clark College
18. Grinnell College
19. Mount Holyoke College
20. Marlboro College

For an index of colleges and universities in the United States that have programs in Lesbian, Gay, Bisexual, Transgender and Queer Studies, or that offer support and resource centers, visit this Web site:

www.queertheory.com/academics/schools/queer_schools_usa.htm

A tremendous percentage of gay teenagers actually begin to explore their sexuality and become more comfortable being gay as they enter into their college years.

Unlike in high school, in many situations you'll find that being gay is more accepted in college, both among faculty and the students. The level of acceptance will vary, based on the school itself and where it's located. Schools in larger cities, in New York, Los Angeles and Boston, for example, tend to offer more tolerance and acceptance than some conservative schools in rural areas.

Whether you choose to attend college full-time or part-time, this is an opportunity to not only obtain a quality education, but to find an accepting and welcoming environment in which you can learn and grow as a gay person.

Gay Bars and Clubs

Every gay bar and gay club, no matter where you are, has its own atmosphere and attracts its own unique crowd. The gay club scene is a culture unto itself. It's one that is accepting of your sexuality, but also one that many find unsatisfying, because the people who get caught up in this scene are often using the clubs as a form of escapism, to get away from their everyday problems — through loud music, sex, alcohol and drugs. In many areas of the country, gay bars and clubs offer the only places where someone can be openly gay with no negative repercussions. This, of course, can be very alluring if you're forced to spend much of your life acting straight to fit in and just survive.

Once you visit a few clubs, you'll quickly discover that there's a very fine line between visiting a club for the pure entertainment value, and getting totally caught up in the gay club lifestyle and sub-culture.

Some clubs, for example, cater to the younger (18 to 24) gay crowd, while others focus on older men or guys who appreciate certain types of music or a fetish. How do you find a club or bar that's right for you? Word of mouth typically works best. However, you can also check out gay club directories online (or in print), then visit the Web sites for specific clubs. Most clubs offer picture galleries on their Web sites, so you can see what type of people the club attracts, how the people dress and what the overall atmosphere is like.

The trick to enjoying the gay club scene is to figure out where you fit in the best. Find a club that plays the music you like and that's frequented by other people around your age, who you'd enjoy hanging out, dancing and socializing with. On various nights of the week, clubs typically offer different themes or special events, which attract very different crowds.

As someone who is new to the gay or mixed club scene, if you're over 21, check out the various clubs in person and see which ones you like best. At first, you may spend a bit on cover charges until you find a club you really like, but think of it as an investment. For the 18 to 21 crowd, your club choices will be more limited, so focus on word of mouth to find the true hot spots.

The clubs that cater to the younger (18+) crowd will be obvious. Even within these clubs, the "rules" for meeting people tend to be different, depending on where you go. As a general rule, however, if you're cute, once you step through the doors of a club, guys will approach you, offer to buy you drinks, and/or ask you to dance.

Overall, the people who frequent gay clubs are pretty friendly. However, there are always exceptions. You'll find that within each club there are close-knit groups of friends or clicks (just like in high school). You'll find sporty jock types, fashion-oriented queens (guys showcasing the latest designer label fashions), drag queens, guys who dance with their shirts off to show off their bodies and everything else in between. Gay clubs tend to attract a wide range of people, all of whom want to dance, socialize and have fun in an environment that's accepting.

The trick to fitting in at a club is to dress comfortably and to convey a confident attitude. If you look cute, act confident and appear to be having a good time, you'll probably get attention. If you're new to the whole club scene, it's best if you go with one or more friends you can hang out with until you're acclimated and learn the ropes. Once you get to know the club's regulars and fit into the scene comfortably, you can go alone to the club because you'll know people once you get there.

In most club (or bar) environments, if you're young, chances are people of all ages will hit on you, especially if you're cute, approachable and appear to be outgoing.

This is not always, the norm, however. If you get hit on by someone who isn't your type or whom you have no interest in, simply say something like, "Thanks, but I have a boyfriend." or "I'm here with someone." If you're bold, you could always go with the honest approach and say, "Thanks, but you're not my type."

While trying to fit in, also try to be yourself and be open to having a good time. If someone offers to buy you a drink, especially if it's an older guy, try to determine what their motivation is. Is the guy being polite and friendly, or is he trying to make sexual advances toward you? By accepting the drink (even if it's a soda), is there some type of implied obligation attached? If you're uncomfortable accepting a drink offer, politely refuse. Say something like, "Thanks, but I don't drink", "I've already had enough, but thanks" or just say, "No thank you."

Photo (c) 2002 Mark V. Lynch, Latent Images

If someone twice your age, for example, offers you a drink and you're at the club with a friend, see if the guy will offer both you and your friend a drink. This could mean he's simply being nice and generous, and doesn't expect anything more than light conversation or maybe a short dance in return. In these situations, it's important to use your instincts.

As you explore a club, if someone catches your eye, try making eye contact. If you make repeated eye contact, have prolonged eye contact or exchange smiles, for example, it could be an opportunity to strike up a conversation or hit the dance floor together.

If the person who catches your eye is already on the dance floor, try walking up to him, say 'hello' and start dancing. You'll be able to tell pretty quickly what the reaction from the guy is. If he's interested, he'll keep dancing. If he walks away, find another guy.

If you're under age, don't try sneaking into a club. If you're caught with a fake ID, chances are you won't get into the club. If you're caught by the police, you'll be forced to pay potentially high fines and could be arrested.

No matter where you are, the gay community is pretty close knit. Thus, it's very easy to develop a positive or negative reputation. If you're seen being overly flirtatious, constantly drunk or leaving the club with a different guy each night, you'll create a negative reputation for yourself quickly. While it takes time to establish a good reputation, you'll find you can trash your reputation quickly and easily, so be careful. Word of mouth travels quickly. It's certainly okay to flirt in a club, but do you want to be thought of as a slut?

At first, the whole gay club scene may seem a bit frightening and extremely strange. After all, it's not everywhere you'll see drag queens, partially naked guys and other gay people all together. The club scene may take a bit of getting used to. Through experience, however, you'll quickly discover how things work. It's very hard to describe the culture and how to fit into it, since the gay club culture is so diverse.

As you prepare for a night at the clubs, set limits for yourself and stick to them. Yes, in most clubs you'll find alcohol and probably drugs. If you're young and cute, you'll be hit on and offered drinks, drugs, sex and a whole menu of other things. But believe it or not, it's totally possible to have an awesome time dancing and socializing without getting drunk, high or artificially stimulated with illegal substances.

For many young gay guys, the club scene offers a place to be themselves, have fun and be accepted. It's a sub-culture unto itself that can be very alluring and somewhat addicting. Even in the most conservative of communities, within a gay club it's okay and accepted for guys to dance together, make out, hold hands and show affection for each other.

Keep in mind, not everyone frequenting a club is there for the same reason as you. Some people you meet will at first seem totally friendly and normal. In reality, they may be on drugs, drunk out of their minds or simply looking to hook up on the spot. It's very common for people to lie (or stretch the truth) about who they are.

Thus, when dealing with strangers, always proceed with caution! Some people at the clubs who see a young and cute guy will stop at nothing to get them. These people tend to be good at what they do, and know the right things to say, because they've been doing it for a long time. While only a small portion of the people at gay clubs fit this description, you must always be observant and trust your instincts. Don't be naive!

Always watch a bartender pour your drink(s), and make sure nobody adds something to them. Also, never leave your drinks unattended in a club or bar.

One way to get the lay of the land, so to speak, when you're visiting a club for the first time, is to strike up conversations with guys who are clearly the regulars, who already know the ropes and who are the popular ones. These hopefully non-jaded guys will often share their information and knowledge with you, and at the same time, being seen with these people will boost your image at the club. Ideally, you'll be accepted faster if one of the established and popular people in the club introduces you around.

The gay club and bar scene can be a wonderful, fun and exciting social outlet, especially if you love music and enjoy dancing in an accepting environment.

One final note of caution, however. In addition to the what may seem like an endless supply of hot muscle studs who spend their days at the gym and their nights dancing shirtless at the clubs, the club crowd also encompasses gay guys who will offer to buy you drinks and may proposition you for sex (possibly in exchange for money) if you're young and cute. While the offer may seem great, accepting cash or even nice gifts to satisfy a lonely guy is not only illegal, but most people will have moral problems with that. Don't be surprised if you're propositioned or approached in a manner that makes you uncomfortable.

In addition to clubs and bars, raves are one of the most popular social outlets among gay teens. According to the official alt.rav FAQ (**www.hyperreal.org/ raves/altraveFAQ.html**), a rave usually refers to a party that lasts all night and that's open to the general public. Loud, nonstop techno or house music is typically played. People may also partake in a number of different (illegal) chemicals, although the latter isn't necessary. At a rave, the deejay controls the party's atmosphere and the psychic voyages of the dancers. The concept behind raves is built upon sensory overload. These parties offer a barrage of audio and often visual stimuli that are brought together to elevate people into an altered state of physical or psychological existence. People attend raves to dance, party and experience the music.

Gay Support Group Meetings

Whether it's a local PFLAG (**www.pflag.org**) meeting or a Gay-Straight Alliance group meeting at your high school or college (or in your community), it's here you'll typically find other young gay people who are looking to make new friends and share their experiences.

The Gay-Straight Alliance Network (**www.gsanetwork.org**) is a youth-led organization that connects school-based Gay-Straight Alliances (GSAs) to each other and community resources. Through peer support, leadership development and training, the GSA Network supports young people in starting, strengthening and sustaining GSAs and builds the capacity of GSAs to: create safe environments in schools for students to support each other and learn about homophobia and other oppressions; educate the school community about homophobia, gender identity, and sexual orientation issues; and fight discrimination, harassment and violence in schools.

According to the network, "A GSA is a student-run club, typically in a high school, which provides a safe place for students to meet, support each other, talk about issues related to sexual orientation and work to end homophobia. Many GSAs function as a support group and provide safety and confidentiality to students who are struggling with their identity as gay, lesbian, bisexual, transgender or questioning."

If your school doesn't yet have a GSA, you can often affiliate yourself with a group at a neighboring school, or start your own group. For information on how to start a group, point your Web browser to:

www.gsanetwork.org/resources/start.html

Gyms / Health Clubs

A large portion of the teen gay community is obsessed with their physical appearance. This may be due to the perception that muscle studs are hot and if you want to be hot, you need to have a perfect body. You do not, however, have to become a muscle stud to be popular or considered hot. You'll probably find that a gym or the fitness center at your college/university is a great place to meet people, socialize and stay physically fit.

The Mall

It's a common stereotype associated with the whole being gay thing: most teen gay guys want to look good. This often comes across in what they wear, their hairstyles and how they take care of themselves from a skincare, exercise and overall fitness standpoint. So, if you're looking for other guys that also want to look their best, it makes sense to hang out and shop at the same places they do.

For teenage gay guys, this could mean frequenting stores at the mall, like Abercrombie & Fitch, The Gap, Banana Republic and Old Navy, for example. It's also a good bet that any guy who buys skincare products at places like Origins, The Body Shop or Aveda is also more concerned about their complexion than your typical straight guy. Is this jumping to conclusions and perpetuating a stereotype? Well, yes. But at the same time, there's no harm in cruising these stores to check out the potential sights.

Theater

Although seeing a show offers a non-interactive environment, Broadway-style shows and musicals tend to attract a gay audience. Likewise, if there is a theater group or choir at school or in your community, participating either on stage or behind-the-scenes is yet another way of meeting gay people.

Gay-Oriented Travel

When the rest of your high school or college friends take off for the most popular Spring Break destinations or take off on trips during the summer, consider traveling to one of the world's gay hotspots. Several cities in America offer large and established gay communities and vacation destinations. Not only are these areas openly gay, you'll find all-gay resorts, restaurants, beaches, clubs and bars in these locales.

Obviously, it's never a good idea to travel alone to a strange city. If possible, bring a friend or a group of friends. As you're deciding where to travel, consider these popular destinations:

Atlanta, Georgia

As one of America's top 10 largest cities, there's a pretty sizable gay population here, as well as a selection of gay clubs, gyms and bars. For details about Atlanta, visit this Web site: **www.gayguides.com/Atlanta.**

Ft. Lauderdale, Florida

Located along the beach in sunny Florida, Ft. Lauderdale has a sizable gay population. However, unless it's Spring Break or the peak summer months, the crowd tends to be older. In Ft. Lauderdale and Miami, you'll find a huge selection of bars, cafés, coffee houses, clubs, beaches and other gay-oriented activities. For more information, visit this Web site: **www.gay-guide.com/gguide.htm**.

Key West, Florida

Known as being a gay community, Key West saw its peak in popularity in past decades, but continues to attract middle aged as well as older gay men. The young crowd does exist, but only during peak vacation periods. Gay resorts, bed & breakfasts and beaches are in abundance here. If you're going to visit Key West, plan on staying at one of the gay resorts. You'll need to be 21+ to visit the gay clubs and bars in the area. For details, visit this Web site: **www.gaykeywestfl.com.**

London, England

With so many great travel deals to London from major cities in the U.S., grab your passport and consider spending a week or so exploring the gay culture here. Homosexuality in London is far more readily accepted than in America. Thus, the gay clubs, like Heaven in London (**www.heaven-london.com**), tend to attract thousands of young and hot guys each night. For details about the London gay scene, visit this Web site: **www.gaylondon.co.uk.**

Major airlines, like US Airways, United, Virgin Atlantic and British Airways, often offer special airfares between the U.S. and London. Also, check out **Priceline.com** and **Travelocity.com** for discounted airfares, no matter where you're planning to travel.

Los Angeles, California (West Hollywood)

There are several cities in California with established gay communities, and the West Hollywood area (near Los Angeles) is certainly one of them. The gay club scene here is known worldwide. Gay-oriented hotels, gyms, art galleries, restaurants, bars, shops and dance clubs are plentiful. In fact, every night in West Hollywood, there's at least one gay club catering to the 18 to 24-year-old crowd. Rage, TigerBeat, Velvet and Club7969 are among the more popular clubs.

In this part of California, straight people are in the minority and seeing people in public who are openly gay is the norm. For details about West Hollywood, visit this Web site: **www.westhollywood.com.**

New York City, New York

America's largest city has its own gay community. While the gay scene in New York City tends to be a bit more low key or underground than in other parts of the country, there's certainly a large selection of gay clubs (like Kurfew, **212-479-7300**) and bars here.

Check out this Web site to learn more: **www.gaynyc.com.** The weekly (free) newspaper, *Gay City News* (**www.gaycitynews.com**), is also an excellent resource.

Provincetown, Massachusetts

This relatively small community overlooks the ocean and is a major gay tourist destination in the spring and summer. Gay-oriented resorts, bed & breakfasts, restaurants, cafes, stores, clubs, art galleries, theaters and gyms make up this area where guys openly showcase their gay pride by holding hands in the streets, for example. This is a great place to visit for a weekend in the summer. You'll find the permanent residents tend to be middle aged, but there are plenty of young tourists.

To discover more of what this lovely New England town has to offer, visit these Web sites: **www.ptown.org** or **www.pinkweb.com.**

From Provincetown, Boston and Providence (Rhode Island) are only about an hour away by car or ferryboat. Both of these cities also have a good selection of gay bars and clubs for the 18+ and 21+ crowd.

San Francisco, California

Within this country, San Francisco is known for having the largest and most established openly gay community. This historic city offers sightseeing, countless activities plus a wide selection of gay-oriented hotels, restaurants, clubs, bars, galleries and other things to experience. This is one city where being openly gay is welcomed and accepted.

To learn more, visit these Web sites:

- Gay San Francisco - **www.gay-sanfrancisco.com**
- QSF Magazine - **http://qsfmagazine.com/qsf/guide/index.html**

Special Tours & Cruises

There's an active gay population in virtually every American city, although some are more underground than others. In addition to the cities mentioned here, there are a handful of gay-resorts, gay cruises and other gay-only vacation packages available through independent travel agencies and tour companies. To learn about some of these vacation opportunities, visit any of these Web sites:

- Gay Travel - **www.gaytravel.com**
- Cruising With Pride - **www.cruisingwithpride.com**

As you look into gay vacation packages and cruises, for example, determine in advance the age range of the other travelers. If you're 21 and the average age of the other travelers is 45, you may want to look for something more age appropriate. Also, when a travel package is referred to as 'All Gay,' this means the entire resort or cruise ship has been reserved specifically for a gay event. A 'Gay Group' vacation or cruise means only a portion of a resort or a group of cabins on a cruise ship have been reserved for gay travelers.

Disney's Gay Days

At the Walt Disney World Resort (Orlando) and the Disneyland Resort (Anaheim, California), every year special Gay Day events are held. While the Gay Day events are not officially endorsed or sanctioned by The Walt Disney Company, they have become extremely popular. For details, point your Web browser to:

www.gayday.com or **www.gayday2.com**

If you're a Disney fan or enjoy theme parks, these are events that shouldn't be missed. The Orlando event is typically held in June, while the Anaheim event is held every October. In 2001, for example, over 100,000 gay and lesbian people attended Gay Day in Orlando, while 10,000 gay and lesbian people attended Gay Day 2 at Disneyland. While the theme parks are open to the public during these events, those participating in Gay Day are asked (but not required) to wear red shirts.

In Orlando, for example, the weekend-long Gay Day events also take place at other theme parks, including Universal Studios Florida, SeaWorld and Busch Gardens. For teens and young adults first getting acclimated to the gay scene, the Gay Day events offer a fun-filled way to meet other gay people in a casual, vacation-oriented theme park environment.

Gay Pride Events

Parades, festivals and other events are held annually in cities across America and around the world. These events celebrate gay culture and are attended by gay, bisexual and lesbian people of all ages.

For information about just some of the various Gay Pride events held worldwide, point your Web browser to: **www.interpride.org**.

Photo (c) 2002 Mark V. Lynch, Latent Images

For up-to-the-minutes news and features relating to the gay community, point your Web browser to www.365gay.com.

Shout Out America

Q: What's the best and worst thing about being gay?

"Now that I'm out, the best thing is that I can be true to myself. The worst thing is that I might never have the white picket fence, the loving wife (or husband) and the 2.5 kids which most people see as being the norm."
- David, 22, Long Island, NY

"Now that I've come out, the best thing is there are no more lies. I don't have to live what other people consider to be a 'normal' life. The worst thing is all of the jokes and wise cracks."
- Luke, 18, Erie, PA

"The best thing is the boys! Boys! Boys! Boys! I love boys! We are fabulous. We're the best dressers, the fiercest performers...We rock! Unfortunately, the worst part is that I'm lonely sometimes, but I get over it."
- Tristan, 19, Los Angeles, CA

"My favorite thing about being gay are the really cute boys! The worst thing is having to deal with the hatred, fear, gay-bashing and discrimination."
- Steven, 18, Seattle, WA

"The best thing is the men. The worst thing is feeling abnormal."
- Alex, 23, McAllen, TX

"My favorite thing about being gay is having sex with men. The worst thing is being subjected to stereotypes. Most people think we're disease-ridden, promiscuous, drug-abusing party boys. We're not all like that!"
- Jared, 21, Miami, FL

Now, That's Entertainment!
Gay-Oriented Movie Suggestions: Take 2

■ **Common Ground** - Three of America's best-known gay writers pooled their talents to create a three-part drama about the changing attitudes towards homosexuality in a small town. Featuring an all-star cast, including Jonathan Taylor Thomas (*Home Improvement*), Brittany Murphy (*Clueless*) and Jason Priestly (*90210*), this movie was made for cable television. (Rated TV-MA, Showtime, 1999)

■ **Billy Elliot** - During the British miners strike of 1984, a talented young boy is torn between his new found love of ballet and the disintegration of his family. He discovers a way out when the local dance teacher offers him a chance to train and audition for the Royal Ballet school. (Rated: R, Universal, 2000, **www.billyelliot.com**)

■ **The Laramie Project** - What happens to an American town when something unexpected, unconscionable and unforgivable rips it apart? What happens to its people when they are thrust into the unrelenting glare of a national media spotlight? And what happens to a community when trust among its own people has been shattered? These are questions answered in this original, made-for-television movie that focuses on the aftermath of the Matthew Shepard tragedy in Laramie, Wyoming. Based on actual events, this is an important film for any gay teenager to watch and understand. (Rated TV-MA, HBO Films, 2002, **www.hbo.com/films/laramie/index.html**)

■ **The Matthew Shepard Story** - The Shepard family worked with producer Goldie Hawn on this factual, made-for-television movie, which originally aired in March 2002 on NBC-TV. To learn more about 21-year-old Matthew Shepard and how he was brutally beaten and tortured to death on October 12, 1998 simply for being gay, visit one of these two Web sites:

• Matthew Shepard Foundation - **www.matthewshepard.org**
• Matthew Shepard Tribute - **www.mattshepard.org**

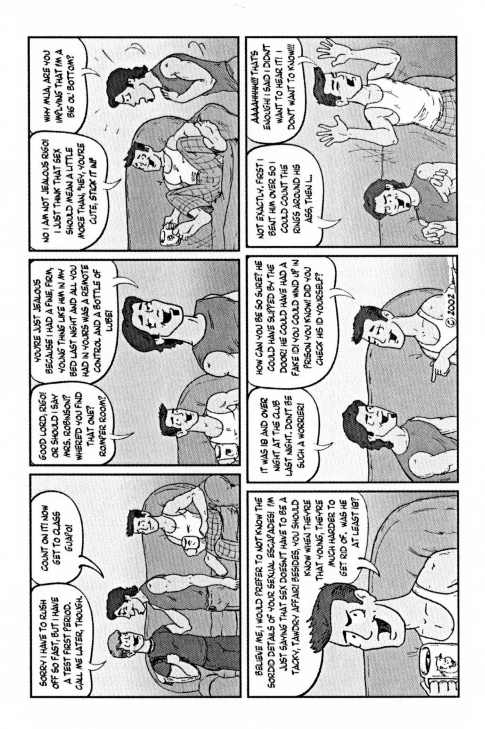

Chapter 5

Relationships:
Boyfriends & Beyond

Okay, you've come to terms with your own sexual orientation (although you probably still have many questions, concerns and even a few emotional issues relating to it) and you've come out to a few people close to you. Perhaps now you're ready to experience another aspect of gay life – dating. Sure, it's great to have friends, but wouldn't it be absolutely wonderful if you had a boyfriend?

There's a big difference between hooking up with random guys you meet at the clubs, for example, and being in a long-term (monogamous) relationship with someone you truly love, respect and enjoy being with.

The first issue you need to address in regard to dating is what exactly you're looking for. If you're young, say, under 16, chances are you're not ready for a long-term and intense relationship. At this point in your life, having close friends, and maybe a casual boyfriend is what you need. For someone who is older, a more serious romantic and loving relationship may help to fill a void in your personal life.

Perhaps eventually, you'll want to go from dating to a more permanent and long-term arrangement. Gay marriages and other long-term romantic relationships are covered in-depth in Chapter 8. However, before you're ready to settle down with someone you love, chances are, you have to meet him first!

So, what are you looking for in a relationship? Something casual (more like a really close friendship)? Do you want to date multiple guys at once and play the field? Are you willing to commit to one special person and date him exclusively? How serious of a relationship are you looking for? Would you consider dating someone who is still in the closet, or who is extremely active in the gay community? What about a guy who is older or younger than you, or who lives in another town, city or state? These are some of the things you'll need to think about. Your answers to these questions will help you determine the best places to meet potential boyfriends.

Just as there's no right time for a gay teenager to come out to himself or to others, there's no perfect time to start dating. It's something you'll want to pursue when you're ready. Being in a relationship involves a commitment. It's not just about going on dates, having sex or spending time with someone. It's all of these things, and so much more.

Photo (c) 2002 Mark V. Lynch, Latent Images

Most gay guys dream of meeting Mr. Right, falling in love and having a wonderful, long-term relationship that's almost like a gay fairy tale. Well, there's no harm in dreaming, but your expectations need to be realistic. Chances are, you're not going to be dating one of those perfect guys from the Abercrombie & Fitch catalog or a Calvin Klein underwear ad.

For a relationship to be truly successful, it needs to be based on a whole lot more than looks and sex. Sure, having a hot boyfriend will offer a tremendous boost to your self-esteem, but it's important to make sure the person you enter into a relationship with has some substance in addition to good looks. A charming personality, intelligence, someone who strives for success and who is well-rounded are just some of the other traits you might want to look for in a potential boyfriend.

You'll quickly discover that every young gay guys says they're looking for a quality relationship, based on honesty, trust and love, but for some people, these are meaningless words used as a ploy to make one night stands and hook ups possible.

When you're ready to start dating, you'll need to gather up your courage, be prepared to take risks (in terms of your emotions) and take steps to meet quality guys you have a lot in common with. Throughout this book, you'll learn many ways of meeting other gay guys, like through the Internet, at clubs or by participating in gay-oriented groups or events, for example.

Dating as a gay teenager is pretty similar to dating as a straight teenager. It's inevitable that until you truly meet the right person, you're going to meet and date people who just aren't perfect for you. Chances are, you'll experience many incredible dates as well as many nightmarish ones. You'll have your heart broken, and you'll probably break a few hearts. Don't despair! Eventually, if you're persistent, you will meet the guy you want to be in a serious relationship with (and who feels the same way about you). In the meantime, have fun meeting people and going on exciting and entertaining dates.

While it's relatively easy for a straight guy to meet girls at school, at camp, on-the-job or wherever they happen to be, for gay guys to meet, it's sometimes a bit more complicated. Not everyone is into the club or bar scene. Thus, as you enter into the whole dating thing, understand it'll probably take some extra effort on your part to meet the right guy for you.

Gay Versus Straight Couples

The biggest difference between two gay guys and straight couples dating is potentially how you act in public when you're together. Straight couples are free to hold hands, kiss, cuddle and express affection in public. Depending on where you live, many gay couples aren't as comfortable showing affection in public.

If you do show affection, you run the potential risk of being starred at, laughed at, harassed or worse. Whether or not you choose to forget about what other people might think and just be yourselves is up to you. You need to decide if you're comfortable and secure expressing yourselves in public. This should be a joint decision between you and your boyfriend.

During your first few dates, this probably won't be an issue, but if you wind up developing a strong affection for someone and dating, you'll want to discuss your comfort level with showing affection in public and decide for yourselves if there's any potential risk involved.

What Do You Have To Offer?

Not everyone is a gorgeous muscle stud or fashion model material. Even if you don't have the absolute perfect body, there's no need to worry! You'll still be able to date, meet great guys, have fun and ultimately find yourself an awesome boyfriend. Before you set off to find and meet Mr. Right, however, think of all of the things you have to offer to someone else. What are your "most marketable" traits when it comes to dating?

Especially if you're shy or have personal insecurities, it's important to truly believe you're worthy of having an awesome boyfriend because you have a lot to bring to the relationship. Next to each of the following categories, write down three qualities about yourself you believe a guy would fall for. If you need help, ask your friends what they like most about you and why.

Physical Appearance
(Example: Physically fit, well-endowed, beautiful eyes, great dresser.)

1.

2.

3.

Personality Traits
(Example: Outgoing, caring, loving, success driven, charming.)

1.

2.

3.

Intellect and Intelligence
(Example: Able to hold conversations on a wide range of topics.)

1.

2.

3.

Morals & Values
(Example: You want to work toward having a monogamous relationship. You only date one guy at a time.)

1.

2.

3.

Social Traits
(Example: Great dancer, loves parties.)

1.

2.

3.

Most Romantic Qualities

(Example: Enjoys romantic walks, quiet dinners for two, cuddling and holding hands.)

1.

2.

3.

In addition to these qualities, what else about you would a guy really like? Are you financially secure or a highly spiritual person? Are you generous and/or willing to place someone else's needs before your own?

Now that you've come up with a list of why someone would want you as his boyfriend, what are the qualities about yourself you believe have the potential to turn a guy off or keep you from dating the guy of your dreams?

Negative Qualities

1.

2.

3.

4.

Based on this list of negative qualities, what can you do to overcome these challenges, change yourself or compensate for them?

Being realistic, out of the things you've listed as negative qualities, how many of these are due simply to your emotional insecurity as opposed to truly being a drawback? Are you being too critical of yourself?

For each of the negative qualities you listed, write down three things you can start doing right now to make these potential drawbacks obsolete or irrelevant to your life. One of the major reasons why people don't wind up in relationships is because they're afraid or too shy to make the first move. Yes, dating can be a scary thing, especially if you've only recently come out and you're first becoming acquainted with life as a gay teenager.

Thanks to the Internet, being shy is no longer a valid excuse for not meeting people. While you may be shy and insecure, so are 99.9 percent of the other guys out there. Now that you've created a list describing all of the reasons why someone would want to date you, there's no reason why you can't be confident about who you are and what you have to offer in a relationship.

One way to build up confidence and self-esteem is to visualize yourself in a quality relationship or on an incredible date. In your mind, see yourself on that perfect date, dressing to impress and showcasing your most lovable attributes. Think about how you'll act, what you'll say, how you'll carry yourself and all of the things you'll do to win the guy's heart. Also, think about some of the things that might go wrong and how you'll deal with them. If you're prepared and have thought things through in your mind, you're more apt to make those positive thoughts a reality.

Remember, you must be willing to demonstrate love, compassion, honesty and be trustworthy as you enter into a relationship if you expect to receive these things in return. You'll only get out of a relationship what you put into it.

Sure, along the way you'll face challenges and have disagreements, but you can't be afraid to communicate from your heart and give of yourself. Don't allow someone to walk all over you or treat you with disrespect. Being in a relationship is an emotional experience, but one emotion you should never feel is fear.

Who's The Perfect Guy For You?

Now that you have a pretty good idea of what you can offer to someone as their boyfriend, ask yourself what you want out of the relationship.

What qualities would someone need to possess for you to consider them the perfect boyfriend? Okay, looks are probably near the top of your list, and that's fine, but dig deeper. What else is important?

Photo (c) 2002 Mark V. Lynch, Latent Images

Attributes of Your Perfect Boyfriend

Aside from their physical attributes, here are a few qualities you might want to look for in a guy:

(Check All That Apply)

- ☐ Athletic
- ☐ Caring
- ☐ Charming
- ☐ Compassionate
- ☐ Confident
- ☐ Creative
- ☐ Cuddly
- ☐ Educated
- ☐ Fashionable
- ☐ Financially Secure
- ☐ Friendly
- ☐ Funny
- ☐ Good Dancer
- ☐ Good Listener
- ☐ Healthy (Health Conscious)
- ☐ Honest
- ☐ Intellectual
- ☐ Kissable
- ☐ Outgoing
- ☐ Perceptive
- ☐ Practical Joker
- ☐ Religious
- ☐ Romantic
- ☐ Smart
- ☐ Spiritual
- ☐ Success Driven
- ☐ Trendy
- ☐ Well-Spoken
- ☐ Witty

Taking his looks (appearance) and all other attributes into account, in 50 words or less, describe your ideal boyfriend.

_____

_____

_____

_____

_____

_____

You now know what you're looking for in a guy. The next step is the most challenging one...finding him!

Finding Your Perfect Boyfriend

Unless you're incredibly lucky, it's going to take a lot of looking and effort on your part to find the perfect boyfriend. Chances are he's out there, waiting to meet you, but you need to locate him. Based on your description of him, where would a guy like that be most apt to spend his time? This is the first place to begin looking.

In the last chapter, you read about many places to meet new gay friends. Well, the same places are where your future boyfriend may be lurking. The Internet is also an incredibly powerful way of finding and meeting potential boyfriends. Chapter 7 offers advice for meeting guys in cyberspace. Be sure to check out the gay-oriented chat rooms, message boards and the on-line personals. Formal dating services are also available to gay guys looking to meet others, but these services don't cater to teens.

One of the very best ways to meet potential boyfriends (and guys worth dating) is through introductions by mutual friends – both gay and straight. Ask around. Make it clear you're looking to meet guys and start dating. You'll be surprised how many people will be willing to fix you up with their other gay friends, cousins, neighbors, coworkers, etc. Also, when you're ready to start meeting guys and dating, rev up your gaydar and keep your eyes peeled!

You'll know you've found the perfect guy when you can't wait to introduce him to everyone you know, as well as take him home to introduce him to your parents. You'll also want to spend as much time with him as possible.

Safety Tip: When you meet a guy for that first time, say, at a club, the laundromat or online, consider giving him only a cell phone number, email address or pager number that can't be tracked back to your home or school address. Also, hold off giving out your last name until you get to know him better. For just a few dollars per month, you can sign up for a pager service that has private voice mail.

The First Date

Once you find a guy you're interested in dating and you exchange phone numbers and/or agree to go on a date, it's time to start planning that all important first date. It's during this time you'll get to know the guy and figure out if he's worthy of a second date.

Whenever you're meeting someone for the first time (or for a first date), there are a few things to consider:

- You want to look your best. Take a shower, brush your teeth, put on deodorant, wear your favorite outfit and style your hair just the way you like it.

- Have an activity (or activities) planned.

- Meet somewhere in public. Until you get to know the guy, don't reveal your home (school) address, get in his car alone or meet at his place. Take things slow.

- Be on time for your date.

No matter what you wind up doing on your first date, be prepared to be social! Whether or not you like the guy, you'll need to keep the conversation flowing until the date ends.

Here are some tips for keeping his attention:

- As much as you want to impress the guy you're flirting with, never lie about yourself. If you get caught in the lie, you'll lose a lot of credibility and that could seriously hurt your chances for developing a romantic relationship.

- Ask questions, listen to his responses and ask related follow-up questions.

- Be yourself! If this person is going to date you, he'll want to get to know you first. At the same time, be on your best behavior.

- Chances are, you're both going to be a bit nervous. That's okay! Try to avoid monopolizing the conversation or babbling.

- Don't be afraid to share information about yourself.

- Make plenty of eye contact! (This doesn't mean stare, however.) If another hot guy walks by, don't let your eyes wonder.

- Pick topics of conversation that are light and positive. Save the serious stuff for later.

- Keep smiling!

- Start a conversation and keep it flowing. Listen to what the guy has to say and respond accordingly. Listening is as important as talking when you're trying to get to know someone.

- Take advantage of your sense of humor. If you can make the other guy laugh and enjoy himself, it'll lighten the mood and help you both relax. Avoid making fun of other people, however. That could easily be a major turn-off.

- Try to be light-hearted, playful and confident with your overall attitude.

- Use your body language to your advantage. Folding your arms across your chest, for example, is anti-social. Gesturing with your hands to make a point, however, helps to convey emotions or add emphasis to what you're saying.

Do your best to be charming and entertaining; try to impress the guy. It may also become your responsibility to keep the conversation flowing, especially if the other guy is very nervous. The trick to this is to be low-key and friendly. Ask lots of questions that require full sentences to answer, not just a 'yes' or a 'no' response.

If you just got out of a movie, for example, you could ask, "Did you like the movie?" Your date might just answer "*Yes*" or "*No*", then you're stuck and will need to bring up a new topic. An alternative is to ask, "So, what did you like best about the movie?" or "What was your favorite scene?" These questions will encourage the other person to voice his opinions and speak openly.

Don't blow your chances with a potentially great guy by drinking too much or doing other things that might be a total turn-off. Also, if you're dining out, be prepared to pay the entire check. Ultimately, you may choose to split the check, but offering to pay is a nice thing to do.

> One of the best things you can do on a first date is through discussion, determine some of the things you two have in common, in terms of interests, hobbies, experiences, likes and dislikes, etc. Maybe you both enjoy the same types of movies or restaurants, or like the same designer clothing. Are you both football fans?

If you really like a guy you're on a date with, one of the biggest mistakes you can make on a first date is jumping into bed with him and hooking up! Are you looking for a one night stand or a relationship? If it's the second, hooking up will probably result in a lack of respect afterwards, plus it makes it harder to get to know him later. A goodnight kiss may be appropriate, but don't rush into anything.

Another common first date mistake is bringing a friend along as a chaperone (this includes a female friend or 'fag hag'). If you're actually on a date and not a group outing, you should be alone with your date (albeit in a public place). If other friends are around, it'll be harder to get to know the guy.

It's true, there are a ton of things to be thinking about while you're on a date. With practice, however, you'll quickly learn how to be yourself, impress the person you're with and discover whether or not the relationship is worth pursuing. At the same time, you'll also enjoy spending time on the dates, getting to know new people and being out with other gay guys in a potentially romantic situation.

Keep The Conversation Flowing

If you're new to the dating scene and shy, this section offers tips for keeping the conversation flowing. As you're getting to know someone, keeping a conversation flowing can be awkward. You don't want too much quiet time, yet it takes a ton of energy to keep the conversation flowing smoothly for a few hours straight during a date. This takes practice. Remember, you're trying to get to know the other person, so ask questions. Also, don't afraid to be yourself.

Your topics of discussion early on don't need to be too intense. You'll find talking about superficial things at first will allow you both to relax and get to know each other. Some of the things you might want to talk about include:

- Books You've Read
- Cars
- Comic Books
- Current Events
- Family
- Fashion
- Friends
- Hobbies
- Jobs / Careers
- Movies
- Places You've Traveled
- School
- Sports
- TV Shows
- Video/Computer Games

A few topics you might want to avoid on your first date are politics, your last boyfriend (why you broke up) and other dates you've had. While you want to share information about yourself, you don't want to talk about yourself too much or come off as self-centered. Make the person you're with the center of your attention. Pay attention to him, look at him and listen to him. During the date, ideally he should be doing at least half the talking.

Great Date Ideas

So, what's on the agenda for your first date? What about subsequent dates? If you're new to the dating scene, the following are some fun date ideas. Some are particularly good if you're on a limited budget. For the first few dates, try to participate in interactive activities that will allow you to talk. Dinner and a movie always works, but see the movie first, so you have something to talk about during dinner.

For the first few dates, agree in advance on the activities. That way, you're sure to do things you'll both enjoy. If you decide to rent a movie, for example, both of you should be involved in picking the movie.

Here are some fun date ideas:

- **Biking or Rollerblading** – Find a park or trail.

- **Camping** – Save this for when you've developed a relationship and you're actually dating.

- **Club** – If you both enjoy dancing, go to a gay club and dance the night away. For a detailed listing of gay clubs around the country, visit **www.gaybars.com** on the Web.

- **Dinner** – You can go to a restaurant for a first date, then make dinner for him at home (or vice versa) on subsequent dates. Picnics are also very lighthearted and romantic.

- **Hiking** – This is a great way to experience each other's company, enjoy the great outdoors and get exercise.

- **Homework** – A study date allows you to spend time with a guy you like and get your homework done at the same time. Just make sure you study your schoolwork and not each other the whole time. (Biology isn't a hands-on course.)

- **Limo Ride** – For a romantic evening, you could drive around in a limo for an hour or two, see the sights and just talk. This is a great romantic touch (although expensive) if you're going to a show or concert together.

- **Lunch** – If you're first getting to know someone, meeting him for lunch, coffee, ice cream or a soda is a lot less formal than a dinner date. It also requires less of a time commitment if you're meeting for the first time and you're not sure if there's going to be a second date.

- **Miniature Golf** – This is a fun and cheap date. It offers light-hearted fun, a bit of friendly competition and a chance to socialize.

- **Movie** – Seeing a movie is always a great part of a date, but you should plan on having dinner or doing something more social before and/or after. Just meeting someone, sitting next to him in a theater, then calling it a night after the movie is hardly a date.

- **Movie Rental** – Once you get to know someone and you're comfortable having him visit your home (or you're comfortable visiting his home), renting a movie can be romantic, especially if you combine it with a homemade dinner or takeout. (Don't forget the micro-wave popcorn!) To set the mood, you might want to dim the lights and light a few candles.

- **Museum / Gallery** – If you want to impress someone by showing you're cultured, consider visiting a muse-um or art gallery. Hey, this isn't for everyone.

- **Play A Board Game** – Instead of just sitting at home with a guy and watching TV, you could so something more social, like play a board game. It may sound a bit cheesy, but it's fun. Twister anyone?

- **Pool** – Add a touch of competition to your date with a game of pool. Many pool halls offer a reasonably good social environment, and it's certainly better than just chilling at a bar (if you're of legal age, of course).

- **Shopping** – There are few better ways of discovering a guy's tastes than by shopping with him. Have him pick out an outfit for you, or you help him choose a new pair of pants. Especially if you both enjoy shopping, a trip to the mall can be a great date.

- **Show / Concert** – Whether it's a Broadway-style musi-cal, a play or a pop concert, if it's something you'll both enjoy, you can plan an entire evening's date around this type of event. Grab a bite to eat, enjoy the show, then maybe go out for dessert afterward. An IMAX movie can also be part of a fun date.

- **Spa Visit** – Okay, this is a bit expensive, not to mention pretentious, but if you can afford it, a trip to the spa can be a romantic and fun date.

Dating Tip: Don't be afraid to let the cheesy romantic side of you show. It's okay to bring your new boyfriend a rose when you pick him up on a date or to send him flowers afterward.

While a dozen red roses might not be appropriate at first, a simple flower arrangement will definitely send the right message. If you're too embarrassed to go to a florist in person in order to send flowers to a guy, you can order flowers online or by phone, from a service like **1-800-FLOWERS** (**www.1800flowers.com**). You'll need a credit card to do this, however.

WARNING!

When on a date, never allow a situation to get out of control. If someone gets too drunk or puts you in a situation you're not 100 percent comfortable with, end the date and leave immediately! It's okay to say "No!" You're never under any obligation to do anything you don't want to do, no matter what.

When Things Get Serious

A good relationship will take time to develop. If you're young and gay, a long-term relationship may last six weeks or six months, instead of years, but whatever the case, there's no need to rush anything. Allow things to happen naturally and at their own pace. Most importantly, always be yourself.

Part of being in a good relationship involves the ability to openly and honestly communicate with each other. Share your thoughts and your feelings. If you both agree it's time to take things to a more romantic level, and you're both prepared for the responsibilities that go along with sharing a higher level of intimacy, than proceed safely. Never compromise your morals, values, level of comfort or health (by participating in unsafe sex) just to appease someone else or as a result of giving into peer pressure.

Relationships are built around love and respect. If someone truly cares about you, they'll wait to be intimate until you're both ready. Before that, however, you may go from casual dating to seeing each other exclusively. This too is a big commitment, but one that will allow you to grow closer since that fear of being dumped for another guy will decrease dramatically.

When Things Go Wrong

Especially if you're young and first getting into the whole dating thing, not every relationship you get into is going to work out. In fact, there are some gay guys who'd swear that men are scum, simply because they've been hurt or mistreated so many times.

If a relationship you're in starts to fall apart for whatever reason, try to figure out what's gone wrong and do what you can to fix it. If you reach a point where the relationship can't be fixed, instead of cheating on your boyfriend and doing things behind his back, you'll avoid a lot of heartache and pain by being open and honest about your feelings and ultimately breaking off the relationship.

Not every guy you meet is going to be faithful, and not everyone will be looking for the same level of committed relationship you may be looking for. When trust and honesty are taken out of a relationship, you've lost extremely important ingredients. Cheating is one of the common reasons why relationships fall apart.

No matter how much you like a guy, the relationship you're in should be one based on love, trust, honesty and respect. If you're being abused mentally or physically, or not treated well for whatever reason, these are definite signs that you need to break up or reevaluate the relationship.

One of the unfortunate facts relating to gay guys dating is that both guys usually bring a lot of emotional baggage into the relationship. After all, it's tough being gay. The challenges gay people face often impact all aspects of their lives, especially on an emotional level. Thus, if one or both people in the relationship is dealing with problems or issues relating to their sexual orientation, this could easily impact the quality of a relationship, especially if one of the people takes out his frustration on the other.

In situations like these, seeking the help of a therapist or counselor is often a good idea. There's no shame in seeking help with relationship problems, whether it's from a close friend, a parent or a professional.

Your ultimate goal in life is to be happy. You may find there are some types of support a boyfriend can't or won't provide. A boyfriend should be an important person in your life, but chances are, he won't be the ultimate fix to all of the problems, concerns and issues you're dealing with. The good news is, you're never too young or too old to find true love and happiness.

Domestic Violence and Abuse

Just as straight couples sometimes have problems that result in one of the people lashing out physically or verbally against the other, domestic abuse also happens in gay relationships. In fact, one statistic revealed that one in four gay men have experienced domestic violence.

No matter how old you are, there is never any excuse to be a victim of violence, especially if it's inflicted by your so-called boyfriend. If you become involved in a situation you can't handle, seek help! Talk with a friend, a therapist, your your doctor, or if necessary, call the police.

The Rainbow Domestic Violence Web site (**www.rainbowdomesticviolence.itgo.com**) reports, "Domestic abuse occurs in approximately 30 to 40 percent of gay and lesbian relationships, which is the same percentage of violence that occurs in straight relationships." Just as with same-sex couples, physical violence can happen in a gay relationship. If there is physical violence in a gay relationship, this can be classified as domestic abuse. Domestic abuse is always about power and control. One partner intentionally gains more and more power over his/her partner.

Domestic abuse can be in the form of physical, emotional or verbal abuse, isolation, threats, intimidation, minimizing, denying, blaming, coercion, financial abuse or using children or pets to control a partner's behavior.

According to a brochure entitled, *Abused Men: The Hidden Side of Domestic Violence,*" published by an organization called Stop Abuse For Everyone (**www.abusedmen.com/brochure.html**), there are several things to look for when determining if you're a victim of domestic abuse.

"If any of the following things have happened to you, you are a man experiencing domestic abuse. If several of the things are happening, you are in severe danger," reports the Stop Abuse For Everyone organization. If you answer "yes" to one, several or all of the following questions (see the next page), seek help immediately and seriously revaluate staying in the relationship.

Another excellent resource is the LAMBDA Gay & Lesbian Anti-Violence Project's Web site (**www.lambda.org/DV_background.htm**). This organization states, "Facing a system which is often oppressive and hostile toward queers, those involved in same-gender battering frequently report being afraid of revealing their sexual orientation or the nature of their relationship."

If you're in a bad relationship, it's important to summon the courage within yourself to somehow correct the situation by seeking the help you and your boyfriend or partner need.

When someone is in a bad relationship, fear is a common emotion. If you're being abused physically or mentally, you need to understand that the person giving the abuse is the one with the problem. You need to protect yourself and pursue a relationship that makes you safe and happy.

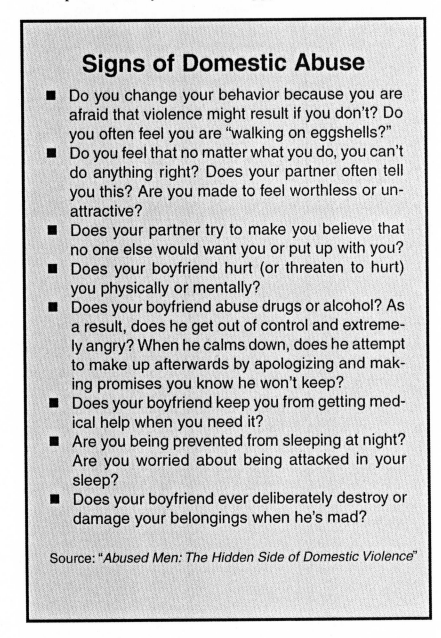

Signs of Domestic Abuse

- Do you change your behavior because you are afraid that violence might result if you don't? Do you often feel you are "walking on eggshells?"
- Do you feel that no matter what you do, you can't do anything right? Does your partner often tell you this? Are you made to feel worthless or unattractive?
- Does your partner try to make you believe that no one else would want you or put up with you?
- Does your boyfriend hurt (or threaten to hurt) you physically or mentally?
- Does your boyfriend abuse drugs or alcohol? As a result, does he get out of control and extremely angry? When he calms down, does he attempt to make up afterwards by apologizing and making promises you know he won't keep?
- Does your boyfriend keep you from getting medical help when you need it?
- Are you being prevented from sleeping at night? Are you worried about being attacked in your sleep?
- Does your boyfriend ever deliberately destroy or damage your belongings when he's mad?

Source: *"Abused Men: The Hidden Side of Domestic Violence"*

24-Hour Domestic Abuse Hotline

If you're in need of help or support immediately, but don't know where to turn, start by calling the **National Domestic Violence/Abuse Hotline**, toll-free at **(800) 799-SAFE**.

This is a 24-hour-a-day hotline that's staffed by trained counselors ready to provide immediate crisis intervention assistance to those in need. When you call, you can be connected directly to help in your community, including emergency services and shelters, as well as receive information and referrals, plus counseling and assistance in reporting abuse.

You can also call this number if you suspect someone you know is a victim of abuse. All calls are kept confidential, and you can remain anonymous if you choose. Abuse can come from a boyfriend, partner, a close friend or even a relative.

Developing Your Independence

Once you hit your teen years and begin dating, you'll probably want to develop more independence and privacy from your parents, friends and others. There are many ways to establish your independence. For example, you could obtain a part-time job (after school and/or on weekends) to begin earning your own money.

With your own money, you can do more of your own shopping, and buy some of your own clothes (in the styles you like), for example.

You might also want to establish your own checking account at the bank, and with it obtain a debit card (which is attached to the checking account). A debit card works wherever Visa or Mastercard are accepted. However, instead of having credit, the money for purchases is taken directly from your checking account, without you having to physically write a check. It also works at ATMs. Some banks allow students to open an account with as little as $50.00.

For more privacy, you might also want your own cell phone (as opposed to a private phone line in your bedroom). You can carry a cell phone anywhere and make/receive calls wherever you are. Plus, depending on the cellular plan and carrier you choose, there are no long distance charges for phone calls. This is particularly useful if you start meeting guys from around the country online, and decide to talk with some of them on the phone.

Cellular and PCS phone companies, like Sprint PCS, Cingular and Verizon, for example, typically offer relatively inexpensive packages (starting around $30.00 per month) that include a predetermined number of daytime minutes, plus up to 3,500 (or unlimited) nighttime and weekend minutes that include long-distance.

Having a cellular phone will allow you to talk privately, without the fear of someone else picking up an extension and listening in on your conversations, plus you'll have your own private voice mail.

If you choose to give out your phone number to guys you meet, providing them with a cell phone number is safer than giving out a home number, because someone can't track down your home address based on a cell phone number.

To help establish your personal privacy, you might also want to purchase a personal digital assistant (PDA) to store your private phone numbers, addresses and other information. Unlike a traditional 'little black book,' for example, a PDA can be password protected, plus you can carry it wherever you go. Palm Computing (**www.palm.com**) and HandSpring (**www.handspring.com**) both make powerful PDAs, starting at prices around $100.00.

Shout Out America
Q: How would you describe the perfect date?

"The perfect date would be spontaneous, romantic, exciting, but definately in an atmosphere where I could be myself."
- Christian, 15, Jupiter, FL

"Watching a great movie, having a nice dinner, sharing a bottle of wine, and then enjoying a sweet night together in bed."
- Jared, 21, Miami, FL

"I like to just hang out. Why does everyone have to go out to fancy dinners and see movies? That's so typical. I like to just spend quality time with the person I'm dating."
- Josh, 18, Atlanta, GA

"A candlelight dinner, complete with romantic music, would start off the date. It would continue with some cuddling, looking up at the stars outside and talking for hours until we fall asleep in each other's arms."
- Kevin, 18, Seattle, WA

"Dinner with a hot boy, a walk along the beach holding hands, then sitting by a fire at the beach at night with the waves crashing around us. This is when we start kissing."
- Tristan, 19, Los Angeles, CA

"A casual dinner alone with my guy, plenty of cuddling and great conversation."
- Joe, 21, Minneapolis, MN

Chapter 6

SEX

WARNING!
This chapter deals with the subject of gay sex in an explicit man-
ner! The information is meant to be informative, not offensive.

You're human – and humans have basic needs, like food, water, sleep and sex. Yes, sex! It's something we all have an instinctual urge for, yet something that for many people is taboo to talk about. Open discussion about gay sex is rare (except among other gay people) and often what's discussed isn't totally accurate.

Safe sex (or what some people call 'safer sex') is an important topic to learn about if you're gay. This chapter, however, also explores the various types of gay (man-to-man) sex and how to better enjoy them.

Sex and Love Are Not The Same

Love is an emotion. It's one that two people have when they care a great deal for one another and perhaps are in a committed relationship. Sex, however, is a physical act. You don't have to be in love to have sex. For a multitude of reasons, people often have sex with people they don't love, and in some cases, whom they barely know or care little about. Is this right? Well, that's for you to decide.

Your sex life is, in fact, your own. You need to determine what's right for you and what you're comfortable with. Ideally, however, you probably want to have a happy and healthy sex life with someone you're in a relationship with (your boyfriend or significant other).

Everyone has their own definition of what sex really is, especially when you're dealing with gay relationships. For some, having sex refers to anal sex or intense sexual relations, but doesn't include kissing, mutual masturbation or even oral sex.

For others, any sensual or sexually stimulating activity falls in the sex category. It all comes down to your personal morals, values and beliefs.

Are you ready to have a sex life? There's no right age to begin having sex. For some, sexual activities begin in their early teen years. For others, it's in their late-teens or early-twenties (or later). The right age to begin having sexual relations with others is when it feels right and you're mature enough to deal with the emotional and physical aspects of a sexual relationship.

Determining when you're ready to be sexually active is an important decision. An equally important decision, however, is choosing the person you want to have sex with, especially if it's your first time. When choosing who you'll have sex with, make sure he's on the same page as you in terms of whatever level of commitment you're looking for.

> As you embark on your sexually active life, keep in mind that relationships (romantic or otherwise) involve love, kindness and trust. Without these elements, you really have very little that's worth anything.

There are plenty of gay guys looking for a steady boyfriend and who would welcome a loving and monogamous relationship with you. There are, however, also 'players' in the gay community who would say or do anything for sex. These people aren't looking for a relationship or commitment. They're just living out one common stereotype of a promiscuous gay lifestyle, hooking up often with whoever happens to come along.

Your body is the most important possession you own and control. If you're going to share it with others, do you want it to mean something emotionally as well as physically? Forget about how other people have treated you in the past, or even what self-worth you give yourself. Before engaging in sexual activities with anyone, you need to understand that you control your body as well as your destiny. It's never okay or acceptable to be disrespected, or to be treated poorly (physically or emotionally) by another person.

Also, understand that few people (if any) are truly happy with their physical appearance. People in their pre-teen and teen years tend to be insecure about their bodies. Even if you're not totally confident about your own physical appearance, it doesn't mean you're not worthy of having a quality relationship. It's okay to be scared and/or shy, but when you engage in any type of sexual activity, it's vital that you're comfortable with the person you're with, as well as with the actions you're about to take.

Relationship or Play The Field?

If you're new to the whole gay scene or young and inexperienced, perhaps you're not yet ready to jump into a serious relationship and have a boyfriend. Even if you're not in a serious relationship, you can still be sexually active.

Choosing to 'play the field' is a personal decision. If this is the path you choose to follow in order to satisfy your social and sexual desires, it's important to always practice safe sex and use a condom, no matter what! You also need to be open with your partners, making it clear you're not pursuing a romantic relationship. How two consenting individuals choose to spend their time is their business.

While this doesn't work for everyone, developing 'friends with benefits' offers an alternative to having a single serious boyfriend.

'Friends with benefits' means you develop one or more friendships with people where the activities you engage in include sexual intimacy, but with no romantic strings. In other words, you're friends, but you hang out, spend time together and can also engage in sexual activities. It's important that everyone involved be on the same page, however, in terms of their true feelings and emotions.

For some people, this type of relationship is more satisfying that simply hooking up with random guys they meet online or at the clubs. Again, it all comes down to choices.

The types of friendships or romantic relationships you become involved in should be based on your own morals, values and personal comfort level.

Young and inexperienced gay teens often wind up believing they've fallen in love with one or more of the first few guys they hook up with. A hook up (one night stand) and a relationship are two very different things, which is why it's important to understand what you and your partner are looking for before engaging in sex.

Get Educated! Act Smart! Be Healthy!

Before proceeding further, there are a few important points that need to be made. First, before engaging in any type of sexual relations that might put you at risk of catching a sexually transmitted disease (STD) or even HIV/AIDS, consult with an expert, such as a doctor or nurse, who can inform you of precautions (not necessarily described within this book).

One of the best resources about HIV/AIDS is The AIDS Hotline (800-342-AIDS). This is a confidential, toll-free number you can call anytime to get your questions answered. Remember, even if you think your questions are obvious or stupid, if you're not 100 percent sure of the correct answer, ask your question!

Never rely on your friends to obtain accurate and reliable information about sex. They're probably more clueless and uneducated about this topic than you are. If you can't easily consult with a medical professional, at the very least, get your questions answered (and your concerns addressed) by doing research online or at the library. Throughout this chapter, you'll be provided with various online resources as well as toll-free phone numbers you can call. Take advantage of these free resources.

> Having sex with another guy doesn't have to be dangerous as long as you take the appropriate precautions.

In addition to being a vast topic with many implications, and one people are extremely uncomfortable talking about, engaging in sexual relations with someone else is a highly personal decision and one that should never be made lightly or while under the influence of alcohol (or drugs). Many believe that sex with other people isn't a hobby or a sport. For you, is it something that should be engaged in arbitrarily? It all comes down to your personal morals and value system.

Within the gay community, it's common for guys to meet at a club or online, for example, and immediately "hook up." This could involve kissing, mutual masturbation, oral sex or something more intense. Gay teenagers especially sometimes become sexually promiscuous for

Photo (c) 2002 Mark V. Lynch, Latent Images

a variety of reasons. This behavior can be highly risky, both emotionally and physically (in terms of catching an STD).

Okay, you're young, healthy, strong and at (or close to) your sexual peak. Thoughts of sex are probably constantly on your mind and you probably spend at least a good portion of your day thinking about sex. That's normal! At the same time, being young, you probably think you're invincible – nothing bad could possibly happen to you. Thus, there's no need to take any precautions when engaging in any type of sexual activities.

Well, you may be strong, healthy and horny, but you're no more invincible than the hundreds of thousand of other gay teen guys who have already acquired and died from AIDS, or who have caught some type of STD that isn't curable. As a gay teenager, you can't ignore the dangers and/or pretend they don't exist!

There are many ways you can deal with your strong sexual urges without putting yourself at risk. It is totally possible to have a happy, healthy and sexually satisfying relationship with another guy, yet be safe.

People will tell you that abstinence (refraining from sex altogether) is the absolute safest way to avoid STDs as well as HIV/AIDS. Well, that's true – but for many, abstinence isn't too realistic.

This chapter deals realistically with gay sex, but it's far from complete. Chances are, you'll still have many questions, so be sure to seek out the appropriate answers before giving into your sexual desires and urges.

AIDS (acquired immune deficiency syndrome) isn't just a gay disease, but it is deadly and gay people are at a high risk of acquiring it if they engage in unprotected sex with someone who is already infected. When someone acquires AIDS, their body's immune system ultimately gets dramatically weakened by HIV (human immunodeficiency virus). Thus, their body can't fight off infections and diseases. HIV infection is increasing rapidly among young people. One reason this age group is at high risk is because of the high level of curiosity and sexual experimentation. One in four new infections in the U.S. occurs in people younger than 22.

STDs (sexually transmitted diseases) can be caught by engaging in unprotected sex (or sexual activities) with an infected person. While not all STDs are deadly, some of them aren't curable. So, if you catch one, you'll be stuck with it for life. More than 12 million people contract STD's every year. Scary, huh?

Sexual Activities

When gay guys engage in sexual activities, this can mean a variety of things. Some of the more popular sex acts include: masturbation, kissing, oral sex, anal sex and BDSM (Bondage & Discipline / Sadism & Masochism).

Masturbation

Solo masturbation involves touching yourself (your erect penis) in order to achieve sexual stimulation and orgasm. Masturbation is a normal and healthy activity that gay, bisexual and straight guys often engage in up to several times per day to alleviate their sexual tension and to get off (achieve orgasm). This activity typically involves using your hand(s) to stimulate yourself sexually. However, various sex toys or objects can also be used.

While masturbating, it's common to fantasize about sex or view pornography, for example. Masturbation (also called whacking off, jacking off or playing with yourself) is typically a private activity done in the shower, in bed or when alone. This activity is healthy (from a physical standpoint), relaxing and can be highly enjoyable.

Some guys, however, find it hot to jack off in front of other gay guys or while engaging in cyber sex (online) or phone sex. Mutual masturbation is when two guys use their hands to get each other off. A circle jerk happens when multiple guys get together to watch each other masturbate or engage in mutual masturbation.

Masturbation Techniques

The most common way guys masturbate is by wrapping their fingers around their erect penis and then stroking it up and down until they reach orgasm. This may be combined with erotically touching other parts of your body, such as your scrotum, pecks, prostate, perineum and/or chest. The perineum is the area between the base of the testicles and your anus. When you're sexually aroused, for some guys, this area becomes highly sensitive.

There are, however, plenty of variations for masturbating. For example, it's possible to rub your erection against something, such as a pillow, your mattress or a sex toy in order to get off. Some guys prefer to use some type of lubricant to make their erection more slippery and intensify the sexual feelings as they rub it.

Does Size Matter?

Men are very sensitive about the size of their penis (when flaccid and erect). The reality is that penises come in all shapes and sizes. There's no such thing as a "normal" size penis. Some studies show that the average penis size (when erect) is between five and seven inches from the base to the tip. The length and width of your penis, however, will not impact your ability to engage in sex or be a good sex partner/lover.

There are some religions that frown upon this otherwise perfectly normal and healthy activity. Thus, choosing whether or not to pleasure yourself (or allow other guys to masturbate you) is a personal decision.

Masturbation Misconceptions

Contrary to popular belief, it's not possible to masturbate too much or too often. You can, however, rub too hard and injure yourself by using excessive force. By masturbating too much, you can't go blind, you won't grow hair on your palms nor will the size of your penis permanently grow (or shrink). Your penis won't fall off either, and masturbation isn't a sexual release just for guys who can't get laid. Oh, and a doctor can't tell by examining you if you've been masturbating. So, if you've been worried about these misconceptions, don't be. If you keep this activity to yourself and clean up when you're done, nobody needs to know you masturbate or how often you do it.

Your testicles (balls) create semen (also called sperm or cum). Periodically, the build up of semen needs to be released. If you don't masturbate or engage in other sexual activities, you may experience nocturnal emission or wet dreams. (This means you ejaculate in your sleep while having an erotic dream). Some guys who don't masturbate will have spontaneous erections (for no particular reason) more often and might ejaculate while doing normal physical activities, without being sexually stimulated. This too is normal, but happens less frequently.

If you remain sexually stimulated for a long period of time without achieving orgasm or release, you could experience "blue balls." This basically is intense sexual frustration that can be somewhat painful. The best way to alleviate blue balls is to ejaculate, either by masturbating or engaging in sexual activities.

Assuming your hands (and genitals) are clean and have no open cuts or wounds, when you engage in masturbation, there is practically no danger of catching an STD or HIV/AIDS from this activity.

Still Have Questions?

One excellent online resource is the Frequently Asked Questions (FAQ) section of The Masturbation Page (**www.masturbationpage.com/asmfaq.html**) or the **alt.sex.masturbation** online newsgroup. The Male Masturbation Techniques Web site (**www.male-masturbation-techniques.com**) also offers 'how to' information, as well as answers to common questions.

More sexually graphic Web sites that deal with masturbation can be found by pointing your Web browser to: **www.skinful.com/malemasturbate.htm** or **www.jackinworld.com**.

Kissing

Obviously, kissing or making out with someone is a way to convey affection. For some people, kissing is more emotional and sensual than participating in actual sex acts. The key to being a good kisser is to use your lips and to relax. Your lips should be soft, pliable, alluring and seductive. Using your lips, you can kiss your partner's lips, or brush your lips gently along their cheek and neck, for example.

Be gentle and sensual! Utilize your breath. Blowing very gently in someone's ear or on one of their body's more sensitive areas can be very arousing. Don't be afraid to be creative as you show affection to your partner.

Massage

Two guys can easily experience intimacy through massage. You don't have to become a Certified Massage Therapist to be able to give an awesome massage. You can, however, pick up a book or watch an instructional video. In addition to being very relaxing, a full body massage can also be extremely sensual or even erotic.

A massage can be purely therapeutic, can be excellent foreplay for sex, or a way of physically expressing your feelings non-verbally to someone else. If you're the one giving the massage, start off gently, using the pads of your fingers and/or your palms as you massage your partner's shoulders, back and/or scalp, for example. Be sure you're in a quiet and private environment and communicate with your partner (verbally and non-verbally) during the massage.

Additional tips for giving a massage can be found online at: www.massagefree.com

When giving a massage, use warm oil or cream to allow your hands to glide smoothly over your partner's body.

Always Practice Safe Sex

Some of the statistics about STDs in this section are downright scary. As a gay guy who may be becoming (or who already is) sexually active, this is information you need to know, however. So please, keep reading!

Engaging in sexual activities and practicing safe sex are two very different things! Sharing sexual intimacy with someone who has an STD or HIV/AIDs could easily result in you getting infected, if you're not careful.

There are more than 20 different types of STDs and not all of them are curable! Right now, more than 31 million people in America alone are infected with at least one STD. Some statistics show that upwards of 900,000 to one million people in

Nearly two-thirds of all STDS occur in people under the age of 25!

Jason R. Rich

America are currently infected with HIV. Anyone can catch an STD. Someone's gender, sexual orientation, race, religion or skin color has nothing to do with it.

In addition to HIV/AIDS, genital herpes, genital warts, gonorrhea, syphilis and chlamydial infection are among the most common STDs.

Unfortunately, without medical tests, it's usually difficult or impossible to tell if someone is infected with an STD or HIV/AIDS. It's important to understand the basics of what STDs are and how they get transmitted.

Some of the more common ways a guy can catch an STD is through unprotected traditional (vaginal) intercourse with a female, anal intercourse with a male, or from licking a dude's penis (oral sex). The person you have sex with must be infected with or a carrier of an STD for you to catch it. Some STDs can also be caught simply from kissing, or from close contact with an infected person's skin, blood, urine, feces or saliva.

According to most experts, HIV/AIDS can not be caught from kissing, sweat, tears, hugging, food, toilet seats, swimming pools or by giving blood.

Photo (c) 2002 Mark V. Lynch, Latent Images

The best way to prevent catching an STD is to avoid sexual contact with others. (Yeah, right! That's probably not going to happen.) If, however, you choose to be sexually active, there are a handful of things you can do to be safer, including:

- Having yourself and your partner tested for STDs before engaging in sexual relations.

- Having regular medical checkups and getting tested for STDs regularly (every few months), even if you show no symptoms, but you've been sexually active with one or more people.

- Participating in a mutually monogamous sexual relationship with someone who is clean of STDs. (In other words, don't cheat on your boyfriend!)

- Using a condom to protect yourself and your partner, especially when engaging in oral or anal sex.

If you suspect you've caught any type of STD, seek out medical attention immediately and carefully follow the protocol prescribed by your doctor. If you don't have a regular doctor (or can't afford one), visit a free medical clinic.

It's true, discussing STDs and sex with a doctor can be embarrassing. However, it's the doctor's job to be understanding, provide confidentiality and offer you answers (as well as medical attention). There's really nothing to be embarrassed about. You might begin by calling a toll-free support number and get some of your questions answered anonymously before seeing a doctor if you're extremely embarrassed.

In addition to The AIDS Hotline (**800-342-AIDS**), you can learn more about STDs by calling the American Social Health Association's (ASHA) toll-free number at **(800) 227-8922**. Online, you can read the National Institute of Allergy and Infectious Diseases / National Institutes of Health's Fact Sheet, called *An Introduction to Sexually Transmitted Diseases*, by pointing your Web browser to **www.niaid.nih.gov/factsheets/ stdinfo.htm**.

The Coalition for Positive Sexuality (**www.positive.org**) is also an excellent and highly informative, yet easy-to-understand online resource about HIV/AIDS and STDs.

The CDC National AIDS Hotline (**800-342-2437/ www.ashastd.org/nah**) handles about one million calls per year – that's about 2,740 calls per day - from people like you who have questions about prevention, risk, testing, treatment and other HIV/AIDS-related concerns. Information specialists are available 24 hours a day, 7 days a week, and can answer questions, provide referrals and send free publications through email and postal mail. This Web site offers links to other useful resources pertaining to STDs.

HIV Tests

Simply by looking at someone, it's impossible to tell if they're HIV-positive (HIV+). Unfortunately, people who are infected sometimes lie, so you can't always trust people who say they're clean. It's also possible for someone to be HIV+ and not know it himself. If you think you've been exposed to HIV/AIDS, get tested!

Home Access Express (800-543-9488 / www.hiv-test.net) and Home Health Testing (800-211-6636 / www.homehiv-test.com) both offer Home HIV Test Kits for about $55.00.

If and when you choose to get tested, you have multiple options. You can take a **confidential test**. This is typically done by your own doctor or medical practitioner. He/she is ethically bound to keep the results of your test a secret from other people. Hence, it's supposed to be confidential. There are some drawbacks to this, however. If you test positive, it is possible your parents, your school, your insurance company and possibly your employer could be notified or gain access to your medical records.

Taking an **anonymous test** is typically the best way to go. You can take this type of HIV test by contacting the local Department of Health, a hospital or local AIDS organization where you live to determine where this type of test is administered. When being given this type of test, you never have to reveal your name, address, phone number, social security number or any other type of personal information. At the time the test is given, you'll receive a secret random number. It's with this number that you later obtain your results anonymously.

Instead of going to a doctor's office or clinic, there are also Home HIV Test Kits on the market. They're typically available at drug stores and pharmacies (or can be ordered via mail order). These tests are completely anonymous, because you administer them yourself.

Most Home HIV Test Kits involve pricking your finger and placing a few drops of blood on a special test card. The card and the instrument to prick your finger with are provided. You then mail the card to a specific company's lab to get tested. The results are available by phone, usually within one week. When calling for your results, you use a special number that's provided in the kit. There's no need to give your name or other personal information.

The Home Access HIV Test Kit includes everything you need to anonymously collect and ship a small blood sample (that you obtain by pricking your little finger) to an accredited laboratory. You'll then receive accurate test results, professional HIV counseling and medical or social referrals 24 hours a day, seven days a week (except holidays). These tests have been clinically proven and certified by the FDA to be as safe, effec-

If you have been exposed to any type of STD, seek out medical treatment immediately!

tive and as accurate as HIV tests administered by doctors, hospitals and health clinics.

If you get tested and the results are positive, don't panic! There is a chance of error with these tests, so have the test done again. Next, seek out counseling from a doctor, the AIDS Hotline or another resource. Chances are, you'll need to begin some type of medical treatment immediately to help prevent HIV from becoming full-blown AIDS.

Assuming the HIV is detected early, there are ways you can lead a productive and healthy life, even though there is no cure for HIV/AIDS at this time.

An HIV test can be done using blood or urine. The Calypte HIV-1 Urine EIA test (or Sentinel HIV-1 Urine EIA test) is very accurate, but a bit less accurate than a blood test. The urine test looks for HIV-1 antibodies in your urine, while a blood test actually tests for the HIV-1 virus in your body. Urine can have HIV-1 antibodies, but not the virus iteself.

Some of the common symptoms you might experience if you're infected with HIV/AIDS are listed here. Be sure to consult with a doctor if you experience several of these symptoms for more than a short while.

Just because you have one or more of these symptoms does not automatically mean you're infected. It means, however, you should be tested, and if necessary, treated. Your symptoms may be a result of something else entirely.

Symptoms of HIV/AIDS

- Rapid Weight Loss
- Dry Cough
- Recurring Fever or Profuse Night Sweats
- Profound and Unexplained Fatigue
- Swollen Lymph Glands in the Armpits, Groin or Neck
- Diarrhea That Lasts for More Than One Week
- White Spots or Unusual Blemishes on the Tongue, in the Mouth, or within the Throat

- Pneumonia
- Red, Brown, Pink or Purplish Blotches On or Under the Skin or Inside of Your Mouth Nose or Eyelids
- Memory Loss, Depression and other Neurological Disorders

Other Common STDs

The following are brief descriptions of common STDs and their related symptoms:

- **Chlamydia** – This is one of the most common and easily spread STDs. Symptoms include a white or watery discharge and pain when urinating. It can cause serious health problems if not treated early. Statistics show that there are between four and eight million new cases of Chlamydia every year. This STD can typically be treated with antibiotics, especially if caught early.

- **Gonorrhea** – One symptom of this STD is a "drip" (discharge) or pain when urinating. In America, more than 400,000 new cases of gonorrhea are reported every year. Penicillin and/or other antibiotics can often be used to treat most forms of gonorrhea.

- **Syphilis** – One of the first symptoms of syphilis is a sore on the tip of the penis, in or near the anus or on the mouth. If not treated, this STD can cause very serious health problems.

- **Herpes** – This STD is caused by a virus and affects more than 50 million Americans – that's one in five people (and most don't even know they have it)! Herpes is not curable, but it can be controlled somewhat through medication. Symptoms include painful sores near the sex organs, anus or mouth. The blisters go away, but may come back at any time. Someone with herpes might also experience a tingling or burning sensation in their legs, butt or genital region. Statistics show that upwards of 500,000 new cases of herpes develop each year in America.

■ **Genital Warts** (also called venereal warts or condylomata acuminate) – This STD is caused by HPV (human papilloma virus). The warts can grow on or around the sex organs or anus. They can be removed in a variety of ways by a doctor. However, once infected, you'll always carry the virus and new warts could appear. More than one million people per year contract genital warts.

■ **HIV/AIDS** – This is a deadly STD caused by a virus. The body ultimately loses its ability to fight off sickness and disease. Many people don't experience symptoms for months or years after initially being infected, yet these people can spread the virus through many forms of sex, blood or by sharing infected drug needles. If you believe you might have been exposed to HIV/AIDS, get tested, then wait three to six months and get tested again (as recommended by your doctor).

Some irresponsible people create rumors about an ex-boyfriend or lover, for example, by saying he has an STD or is HIV+. This may be used as a form of revenge after a relationship goes bad. Spreading this type of false information about someone else is cruel, potentially damaging and immature. Don't start believing rumors about other people until you've checked out the facts for yourself!

■ **Hepatitis B** – This STD may have no visible signs or symptoms, but it can be spread without the infected person knowing it. Hepatitis B attacks the liver and can cause serious illness. While there is no cure, Hepatitis B can be prevented with a series of shots.

■ **Crabs and Scabies** – Especially among young people, this is a common STD. It involves tiny bugs (yes, little creatures) that cause itching. This STD is spread by close physical contact, or from bed linens and towels. Crabs are found on hairy parts of the body, while scabies live under the skin. Both can be controlled and cured with proper medical attention.

Always Use Condoms

Aside from abstinence, condoms (also called rubbers or prophylactics) are one of the best ways to protect yourself against STDs and HIV/AIDS. Be sure, however, to **always use latex condoms** (since lambskin condoms do not block HIV and STDs and Polyurethane condoms tend to break more easily than latex condoms).

As you'll quickly discover, there are dozens of different types of condoms. They come in different sizes. They're made from different materials. They're available in different colors, and yes, some of them are even flavored or glow in the dark.

The Trojan Condoms Web site offers detailed descriptions of its various condom products and offers a questionnaire to help you select the right condom. They'll even send you free samples!

www.trojancondoms.com

When choosing your condoms, remember its first and foremost job is to protect you, not look cool or taste good. Choose the type of condom you use based on what type of sexual activity you're most apt to be engaging in. If you're having man-to-man anal sex, a pre-lubricated latex condom that fits you well is probably best.

Experts agree that condoms should be worn when engaging in oral sex or anal sex with another guy. If you're using a sex toy, such as a dildo, either put the condom on yourself or on the dildo to keep things more sanitary. (To be safe, don't share sex toys, such as dildos, with others.) Many people opt to not use a condom when engaging in oral sex. This increases the danger of contracting an STD, but is a personal decision.

Not being prepared (and not conveniently having a condom when you need one) is not a good reason to engage in unsafe sex. Make it a strict policy not to engage in any sexual activities without proper protection – no matter what!

In addition to the lubrication that may already be applied to the condom, you can purchase water soluble lubrication (lube) separately. Most drug stores, pharmacies, convenience stores, supermarkets and sex shops carry KY Jelly, for example. Other popular lubes are Astroglide, Aqua Lube, Wet, Foreplay and Probe. Never use Vaseline or petroleum jelly as a lubricant. In addition to being hard to clean up, petroleum jelly will destroy a latex condom.

If you're too embarrassed to go into a store to buy condoms (and lube), using a major credit card, you can order them online. Many gay clubs and school medical centers distribute condoms free of charge. Some clubs, bars and restaurants have condom vending machines in the men's restroom. To get exactly the condoms you want and need it's best, however, to buy them from a retail store, via mail order or online.

It's true, with so many different types of condoms on the market, choosing the right one can be confusing. You can always ask your doctor or the local pharmacist for advice. One way, however, to learn what's available, without dealing with having to ask embarrassing questions at a local pharmacy, is to go online and visit the various condom manufacturers' Web sites.

Make sure the condoms you purchase (especially if you're buying via mail order or online, have the FDA's seal of approval on the packaging). All condoms sold at retail stores have this approval.

Condoms with spermicide don't kill HIV/AIDS. The condom itself will protect you, but the spermicide is used as extra protection to keep a woman from getting pregnant. It's not a disease killer.

Most people are more apt to use a condom if they have one handy when the moment is right. After all, you don't want to break up a romantic moment with a trip to the pharmacy. If you're going to be engaging in sexual activities, plan ahead and have a stash of condoms on-hand. Keep them near your bed, in your wallet, in your car or wherever they'll be handy when you need them.

There are many common excuses for not using a condom, including lack of knowledge and lack of availability at the time they're needed. No matter what your excuse is, not using a condom when engaging in sexual activities can be extremely dangerous for you and/or your partner!

Putting On and Using A Condom

If you've never used a condom, before engaging in sexual relations with someone else, go to the store, pick up a few different types of condoms, try them on and learn how they work. Read the directions carefully that come with the condoms you buy.

The following are some basic tips for buying and using a condom:

■ Choose the right type of condom for your needs. Make sure you choose the right size, if applicable. Sure, everyone wants to wear an 'extra large' condom, but if it's too big it won't work properly. Likewise, if a condom is too small, it will cause discomfort.

■ Check the expiration date on the packaging and make sure the condom hasn't been tampered with. All of the packaging should be factory sealed. Even if a condom is still in its original packaging, if it's been exposed to extremely hot weather, carried in your wallet for a long time or has been accidentally washed with your laundry, throw it out and use a fresh one.

■ Once you've acquired a condom and you're ready to use it, open the packaging and remove the condom. Tear the packaging carefully – you don't want to rip the condom itself.

■ To place the condom on, your penis must be erect (hard). If your penis is uncut (uncircumcised), pull back the foreskin before putting the condom on.

■ Make sure the condom isn't inside out.

■ The condom should roll easily onto your erect penis. Hold the tip of the condom with your fingers as you roll it in order to keep out the air bubbles. At the tip, there might be a small reservoir to catch your sperm (cum) once you ejaculate. The condom should be rolled down as far at it'll go (toward the base of your penis, near your scrotum).

■ Once you've used the condom (and have ejaculated into it), take it off by unrolling it, then throw it away or flush it down the toilet. **Never** wash the condom and re-use it, or give it to someone else to use!

■ Practice putting on and removing a condom in a private place if you've never used one. The condom should fit a bit snugly so it won't fall off, but it shouldn't be too tight or painful.

For a pictorial guide on how to use a condom, point your Web browser to: http://sweetecstacy.com/tutorial/howtocondom1.htm

Using a condom correctly and faithfully isn't a big deal. They're cheap, readily accessible and easy to use. Most importantly, they'll help to keep you healthy and safe. If you're too embarrassed to purchase condoms, even from a convenience store or pharmacy where nobody knows you, you're probably too immature to be having sex.

Oral Sex

Kissing could be considered a type of oral sex. However, most gay people think of oral sex as involving blow jobs or rimming. Unfortunately, there's no accurate answer about how safe oral sex is in regard to HIV/AIDS. However, if someone has other STDs, such as genital warts or herpes, for example, whether or not their symptoms are obvious, these and other STDs can be caught from engaging in unprotected oral sex.

Herpes is one example of an STD that can be easily contracted by skin coming into contact with an open herpes blister (which may, or may not be visible). Thus, kissing someone with herpes or engaging in oral, anal or other type of sex could be risky.

When giving oral sex to someone else, if you refrain from swallowing their cum (semen), this reduces some risk. However, the only safe way to prevent HIV/AIDS is to have the person receiving a blow job wear a condom.

A blow job involves one person licking and/or sucking on another dude's penis in order to administer intense sexual pleasure. Rimming involves licking in or around your partner's butt hole. This feels great for the recipient, but is highly risky from a health standpoint, especially if one partner has an STD.

Question: Can you get HIV from performing oral sex? According to AIDS Partnership Michigan, the answer is an unequivocal 'Yes!'

Research shows there have been a few cases of HIV transmission from performing oral sex on a person infected with HIV. While no one knows exactly what the degree of risk is, evidence suggests that the risk is less than that of unprotected anal or vaginal sex.

It's possible that blood, semen, pre-seminal fluid, and vaginal fluid all may contain the virus. Cells in the mucous lining of the mouth may carry HIV into the lymph nodes or the bloodstream. The risk increases if you have cuts or sores around or in your mouth or throat; if your partner ejaculates in your mouth; or if your partner has another sexually transmitted disease (STD).

Using a condom during oral sex greatly reduces your risk of becoming HIV-infected if your partner has the virus.

Anal Sex

Anal sex involves intercourse between two guys. One partner inserts his erect penis, a sex toy or his finger(s) into the other person's anus. This typically provides sexual pleasure for both partners.

The person who inserts his penis into his partner's butt is considered the 'top,' while the partner on the receiving end (so to speak), is referred to as the 'bottom.' During this activity, the top receives sexual stimulation from his penis rubbing against the walls of his partner's anal canal or against his partner's prostate. The bottom receives pleasure from having his prostate rubbed and stimulated.

Not all sexually active gay people engage in anal sex. After all, someone's butt is not the same as a woman's vagina. Some guys find anal sex disgusting and painful, while others find it intense and enjoyable. This is the riskiest aspect of gay sex, whether or not you use a condom for protection.

The **prostate** is a gland located in the center of your pelvis. It's highly sensitive to sexual stimulation. During erotic stimulation, the prostate becomes increasingly aroused. About 1/3 of your ejaculate comes from the prostate. It can be stimulated externally or through the anus.

In addition to the possibility of STDs, there are other risks involved with anal sex, especially if it's rough. Plenty of lubricant should always be used and the person on the receiving end (the bottom) should be in control and very relaxed. If not performed safely, aside from STDs, possible complications include bleeding, pain, perforation of the colon wall and in rare instances, incontinence (the inability to control one's bowels). For more information about anal sex, point your Web browser to **www.gayhealth.com**.

Sexual Fetishes

A 'fetish' involves getting extremely turned on sexually from a specific activity or type of visual stimulation. There are many types of fetishes. As long as both partners act safely, are consensual and play by the predefined rules, there's no harm in exploring sexual fantasies or fetishes.

Types of fetishes include: bondage, spanking or tickling. People also have foot fetishes; medical festishes (where they fantasize about doctors or nurses engaging in sexual activities with them); leather or rubber fetishes (where the partners wear leather or rubber clothing during sex); a passion for water sports (sex involving water or piss); or underwear fetishes (guy's in sexy underwear or jockstraps are a major turn-on).

A fetish can also be for a person with a specific look, such as blonds, jocks, muscle studs, smooth guys, hairy guys or twinks, for example.

As long as you're not hurting anyone (physically or emotionally), exploring your sexual desires and fetishes can be a healthy and normal expression of your sexuality.

Consensual Sex

In any sexual relationship, the partners **must** both be consensual. Forcing a gay or bisexual guy to engage unwillingly in sexual activities is rape, just as it is with a guy and a girl.

Rape, date rape and other forms of non-consensual sex occur among gay people, just as they do with straight people. The age guys can legally engage in sexual relations varies by state. There are laws that protect young boys from being molested or sexually abused by older guys. In every state, the legal age of consent is different.

For information about age of consent laws in your state, point your Web browser to **www.ageofconsent.com** or **www.avert.org/aofconsent.htm**.

Do You Have To Date Guys Your Age?

Of course not! While there are laws prohibiting adults from engaging in sex with minors, you're free to date guys who are younger or much older. In fact, it's common and perfectly normal for teen guys to be attracted to people who are older or even a few years younger.

While most 17-year-olds don't have a lot in common with 40-year-olds, for example, you may meet a younger or older guy with whom you share a special bond, common interests and a sexual attraction. If you're both getting happiness and pleasure from the relationship, there's probably nothing wrong with pursuing it.

Being involved in a relationship with someone who is older or younger is okay, as long as you're both happy, healthy and safe, and you're both getting what you need out of the relationship from an emotional as well as physical standpoint.

The Secret To Great Sex

The secret to great sex is to be open and honest with your partner. Be safe and always communicate. Figure out what your partner likes and dislikes, and what really turns him on. Develop a strong sense of trust with your partner.

Great sex is about love and intimacy, not just getting off. You'll quickly discover that sex with someone you truly care about is far better than hooking up with random guys. As you grow closer to your partner, don't be afraid to experiment and try new things. After all, sex is supposed to be fun!

Never be forced into anything (a situation or a sex act) that makes you uncomfortable, especially with someone you've just met. Most importantly, be mature and responsible! If you're not ready to engage in sexual activities, hold off. Do what makes you feel comfortable,

Photo (c) 2002 Mark V. Lynch, Latent Images

and don't worry about living up to someone else's expectations or living out what you believe is the gay stereotypical lifestyle.

Be yourself! Be safe!

Chapter 7

Gay Life
In Cyberspace

Shout Out America
Q: Are you concerned about HIV/AIDS and other STDs?

"Of course STDs are a concern. The best way not to catch anything is to do what I do. Not sleep around!"
- David, 22, Long Island, NY

"If you know how to protect yourself and you're careful, there's no reason to be concerned."
- Gerard, 25, Washington, DC

"I'm very concerned. What do I do to protect myself? Condoms! Condoms! Condoms!"
- Bryan, 22, Orlando, FL

"Always play safe! Use protection!"
- Joe, 21, Minneapolis, MN

"Always wear a condom, no matter how drunk you are. It only takes one time to mess up your life forever."
- Tristan, 19, Los Angeles, CA

"I'm not having sex until I know I've found the right guy."
- Josh, 18, Atlanta, GA

"Of course I'm concerned! I always use condoms and won't do more than oral sex until I know for sure if a guy I'm with is clean and disease free."
- Luke, 18, Erie, PA

"I'm very concerned about HIV/AIDS! I don't mess around with people. I stay true to myself and my religion."
- Christian, 15, Jupiter, FL

Jason R. Rich

Years ago, for a closeted gay person to interact with other gay people, it was extremely difficult, since there were so few ways for gay guys to meet.

Using the Internet, it's now possible for you to easily and privately explore your sexuality in cyberspace, gather information and communicate with others. While kicking back at home or in your dorm room, it's possible to:

- Gather information about gay-related issues and topics
- Send and receive email
- Chat (live) one-on-one or with groups of people with similar interests
- Use a Web cam (videoconferencing) to communicate with text, voice and pictures with other gay people
- View gay pornography - XXX-rated material, if you're over 18 (21 in some states)

No matter what time of day (or night), the Internet can connect you to other gay people with whom you can share ideas, explore your sexuality, make friends, exchange information and possibly even meet your next boyfriend. Oh, and if you have questions about your sexuality, answers are just a few clicks of the mouse away.

For gay teenagers, the Internet offers several major benefits. It's available 24-hours-per-day, everyday, plus it's possible to gather information and communicate with people anonymously, using a made up persona, or as yourself. So, if you're still in the closet, you can stay there, but still interact with the large and diverse gay community that's active online.

If you're a gay teenager and you're not online, you may really want to see firsthand everything that's available on the Web! If you don't own a computer, find a way to obtain access to the Internet, preferably in a private environment if you're still in the closet.

In addition to offering information about gay-oriented Web sites, chat rooms and online resources, this chapter explains ways to keep your surfing a secret from others by covering your tracks if you're still closeted and don't want your parents, for example, to figure out where you've been surfing on the Web or who you've been communicating with. You'll also discover how to set up a free, private email address which can be accessed from any computer that's connected to the Web.

While the Internet is a wonderful tool for communicating with other people (without actually coming out to your friends and family), there are potential dangers that lurk in cyberspace. For example, there are creeps in cyberspace who create false identities in order to lure young and unexpecting gay teenagers into compromising and sometimes dangerous situations. In other words, someone with a screen name or online profile that describes himself as a hot teenage guy could be a sex offender or rapist in search of his next victim.

As you'll quickly discover, there are a few important rules to remember when communicating with others online, especially if you're a closeted gay teenager. People aren't always who they appear to be when you're communicating in chat rooms or via email.

If you're trying to remain anonymous, create a separate email account (using Hotmail, for example) and a separate AOL Screen Name (if applicable) for yourself. How this is done and why you should do this will be explained later.

> **Never (no matter what) reveal your full name, address, home phone number, computer passwords or any personal information to a stranger you meet online!**

<header>
Jason R. Rich
</header>

Getting Yourself Online

There are many ways you can get yourself online. Ideally, a personal desktop computer or laptop computer (equipped with a telephone modem or high speed Internet connection) should be used. However, there are also wireless PDAs (Personal Digital Assistants), pagers, cell phones and even set-top boxes (like WebTV) that connect to a television set and offer access to various aspects of the Internet. These days, even some home video game systems can be used to access the Web.

If you don't have access to the Internet at home, most schools, public libraries and Internet cafés offer Internet access, but in a less private environment. In addition to access to the Internet's World Wide Web, there are millions of gay people who belong to America Online (AOL), the world's largest online community. Those who aren't AOL members can still utilize AOL Instant Messenger to communicate with others, but more on that later.

Access to the Internet typically costs between $9.95 and $49.95 per month, depending on the type of connection and service you use. Once you're online, you can surf the Web (visit Web sites), chat and send/receive email.

When you subscribe to an Internet Service Provider, you'll be given an email address (or in the case of AOL, a Screen Name and email address). Since this is your online identity, you'll probably want to share it with friends, family and others, who may or may not know you're gay. Thus, to remain anonymous or to keep your online gay life separate from your online closeted life, creating separate email addresses and/or AOL Screen Names is a good idea.

Hotmail (**www.hotmail.com**) and Yahoo Mail (**http://mail.yahoo.com**) are two services that allow you to set up free email accounts that you can access from any computer that's connected to the Internet. Your Screen Name and/or email address, as well as the profile you create, is how people will know

- 169 -

you. Thus, if you're looking to meet other guys, a catchy screen name always helps. Without revealing your last name, address, phone number or other details that someone could track you down with, you'll want to create an online screen name and profile that will encourage others to interact with you.

Your online profile might contain the following information:

- First Name
- Age
- City (Don't Be Too Specific)
- Physical Description (Height, Weight, Hair/Eye Color, Build and Other Measurements)
- Hobbies

Be sure to check out the profiles of other people to learn some of the lingo and abbreviations used. For example, this is how someone might describe themselves when using Gay.com's free Chat service:

```
Screen Name (or first name), M22, brown hair/eyes,
5'8", toned, smooth, cute and str8 acting.
```

Based on this short profile, anyone can quickly determine that this person is a 22-year-old guy (M22), who is five-foot-eight-inches tall, with brown hair and eyes. He's toned, has little body hair, claims he's cute and acts "straight." You'll discover that in addition to creating a somewhat revealing profile, guys tend to be clever when creating their screen name.

Using America Online, you can create a more detailed profile by entering the AOL keyword 'My Profile.' Have some fun and use your creativity as you create your screen name, email address and online profile.

If your first name is Tristan, you could create a boring screen name, like 'Tristan1234', for example, and have the email address Tristan1234@hotmail.com. The screen names 'Tristan-CuteBoi18' or 'TristanJockBoi', however, are more creative and will probably get more attention. Be creative, but be honest.

Keeping Your Online Secrets

If you know anything about computers, you probably know that the popular Web browsers (Internet Explorer and Netscape Navigator) as well as America Online are designed to keep track of what Web sites you've visited, what email you've sent/received and what pictures (and files) you've downloaded. Thus, anyone who accesses your computer after you do can easily discover what you've been doing online.

The good news is, by taking a few precautions, you can keep your Web surfing habits a secret, even from spying friends and parents. So, if you're active in the gay chat rooms, but need to keep this a secret from your parents, this is possible. Unfortunately the following strategies aren't fool proof, but they'll probably keep people who aren't total computer geeks from discovering what you do online.

In addition to the precautions described here, you can also purchase special programs designed specifically to cover your tracks in terms of what you do on your computer. One program is The Surfer Protection Program ($24.95). You can download a free, 30-day trial version of the software from the company's Web site (**www.surferprotectionprogram.com**).

Clean Browser (**www.clean-browser.com**) is a similar package that will clean your Web browser's cache, history folder; cookies folder, clear the drop-down address bar; and erase other related files. To find other programs, use the search phrase 'browser privacy software' with any online search engine.

Web Browser Privacy Tips

Once Internet Explorer 6.x is loaded, access the Tools pull-down menu and select Internet Options. Within the window that appears, you'll see an option in the Temporary Internet Files sub-window that allows you to Delete Files and Delete Cookies. Click on these options. Also click on the Clear History icon. By taking these steps at the end of each Web surfing session, you'll be able to keep casual computer users from discovering what you've been doing online. Netscape Navigator offers similar features to erase your tracks once you're done surfing.

Remember, you want to delete all 'Temporary Internet Files', items in your 'History' folder, new items in your Cookies folder and all other files you downloaded during your surfing session. As you delete files, make sure to also empty the Recycle Bin (if you're using Microsoft Windows).

When downloading pictures or other information from the Web, it's best to avoid storing these files on your computer's hard disk. You might want to save these files on floppy disks or on ZIP disks that you can keep away from those who don't know you're gay.

Privacy Tips for AOL Version 7.0

When using AOL Version 7.0, you can cover your tracks using the 'Download Preferences' and 'Filing Cabinet' features as well as the 'Mail Preference' options, all found under the 'Setting' pull-down menu. You can create and edit your Profile using the AOL keyword 'My Profile.'

Jason R. Rich

Finding Information Online

As someone who is young and gay, you're probably first starting to explore your sexuality and are still discovering what it means to be gay. Perhaps you have explicit sex-related questions you're too embarrassed to ask your parents, friends or doctor about. Maybe you're curious about various aspects of gay relationships, or you have a question about sexually transmitted diseases.

Whether you have questions that need accurate answers, you're looking to learn from the experiences of others or you need support because you're feeling alone, depressed and/or afraid, there are literally thousands of Web sites you can turn to for information. In addition to the online resources described throughout this book, be sure to use any Internet search engine, such as Yahoo! (**www.yahoo.com**), Ask Jeeves (**www.ask.com**) or Google (**www.google.com**), to help you find the information you're looking for.

Want to share your photo online and make it easy for people to find? Check out Facelink.com (www.facelink.com). This is a service that allows you to create your own "FacePage", which displays your personal photo and a short biography. Once you register, you upload your photo, and quickly make a place for your face on the Web. The process takes about two minutes..and it's *free*!

Once you're signed up, FaceLink sends you a short, convenient web address you can place on your email signature, or anywhere else you'd like to add a personal touch. As you're chatting online, you can send people to this link so they can see your face. You can also check out other people and search for hot guys that match your criteria.

Online Gay Information & Support

The following is a short list of useful Web sites worth checking out in order to learn more about topics of interest to gay teens:

Gay, Lesbian & Straight Education Network
(Online Support Network)
www.glsen.org

Gay & Lesbian National Hotline
(Online Support Network)
www.glnh.org

Gay.Com
(Online Community/Magazine) .
www.gay.com

PFLAG
(The Support Group's Official Web Site)
www.pflag.org

Planet Out
(Online Community/Magazine)
www.planetout.com

The America Foundation for AIDS Research
(Information & Research)
www.amfar.org

Trevor Project
(Suicide Prevention/Depression Hotline)
www.thetrevorproject.org

XY Magazine
(The Online Version of the Print Magazine)
www.xymag.com

Gay Chat Rooms

An online chat room is an area where people meet in cyber-space and type text messages (in real-time) to one another. This is the best and quickest way to meet other gay guys online, and it's fun!

There are public chat rooms, where dozens of people from all over the world communicate simultaneously, plus there are private chat rooms where you can talk (type) one-on-one with someone you meet online.

America Online's online chat community also features hundreds of special interest chat rooms where people gather at all times of the day and night. Within AOL's chat room area, you'll typically find special interest chat rooms catering to various gay audiences. Using AOL version 7.0, you can see a complete list of chats happening at any given time by following these steps:

- Once you've logged onto AOL, click on the Chat icon (near the top of the screen).

- Within the Chat sub-window that appears, click on the 'Find A Chat' icon.

- Next, click on the 'Created By AOL Members' icon that appears in the Find A Chat window.

- On the right side of the 'Find A Chat' window is a sub-window listing the names of various chat rooms. Find one that looks interesting and double-click on the name to enter that room.

- AOL chat rooms only hold 23 people each, so if the room you choose is full, you may need to wait for someone to leave. By clicking on the 'Who's Chatting' icon (below the list of chat rooms) you can see a list of the people currently in the room. From this list, you can access their Profiles and send Instant Messages (IMs) to them. An Instant Message is a private message you can send to other AOL members or those who have the free AOL Instant Messenger software (www.aol.com).

- The 'List More' icon below the list of chat rooms will allow you to scroll down the complete list of chat rooms created by AOL members.

How will you know which chat rooms are gay-oriented? It's easy; go by the name! Here are potential names for gay-oriented chat rooms: BostonM4M, MuscleM4M, M4M 18 YRS OLD, M4M18, STR8 BI CURIOUS M4M or STR8 ACTING JOCKS. Keep in mind, while some guys will just want to chat online in order to meet new friends, others will be looking for cybersex, to hook up (in person) or for phone sex.

Gay.Com

It's A Great Online Meeting Place

One of the world's most popular gay-oriented online chat areas is offered by Gay.com (**www.gay.com**). From the main page of this site, click on the 'Chat Now' link located in the upper-left corner of the screen, then choose which chat room you'll like to participate in.

You'll find that Gay.com offers separate chat rooms for various cities across America, plus chat rooms for specific audiences, like gay teens (look for the 'Young Adult 18-24 Only' room). Before entering a chat room, you'll need to create a User Name and a one-line Chat Bio. No matter what time of day or night, you'll always find at least 10,000 gay guys chatting within the various rooms on Gay.com.

For many people, meeting guys online is much easier than at a club or in most other situations. After reading someone's profile or chat bio, simply send the guy an instant message saying, 'Hey, what's up?' and allow the conversation to flow from there.

Early in online conversations, people talk about general things. If you need some ideas about how to keep a conversation going (without getting dirty), some suggestions are offered here. Once you get to know someone, you can get more personal and talk about deeper or more intimate topics. If you're planning to take the cyber sex route, you can always go with all too common line, 'Hey, what are you wearing?', then go from there.

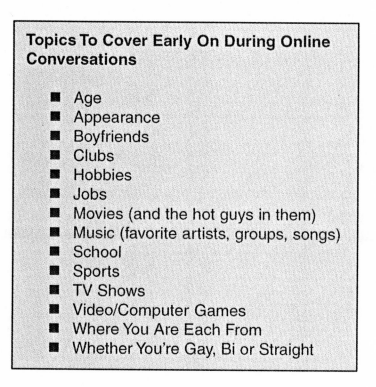

Topics To Cover Early On During Online Conversations

- Age
- Appearance
- Boyfriends
- Clubs
- Hobbies
- Jobs
- Movies (and the hot guys in them)
- Music (favorite artists, groups, songs)
- School
- Sports
- TV Shows
- Video/Computer Games
- Where You Are Each From
- Whether You're Gay, Bi or Straight

Other gay-oriented chat rooms include:

- Gay Teen Chat - **www.gay-teenchat.com**
- Gay Teen Meeting Place
  http://gayteenmeeting.tripod.com
- Teen Gay Chat - **www.xchatrooms.com**
- Yahoo Chat – **http://chat.yahoo.com**
- XY Chat (The under-18 crowd tends to hang out here)
  www.xymag.com

Online chats are text-based. You type messages to people and they type back – all in real-time. When communicating, you'll discover that people use a kind of online shorthand to communicate, since not everyone can type too quickly. Emoticons and abbreviations are also used to convey emotions.

Popular Chat Abbreviations

<G>	Grin
<J> or JK	Joking
<Y>	Yawning
A/S/L	Age, Sex, Location?
BFN	Bye for Now
BRB	Be Right Back
FYI	For Your Information
LMAO	Laughing My Ass Off
LOL	Laugh Out Loud
OIC	Oh, I see
TTYL	Talk To You Later
OMG	Oh My God!

Exchanging Photos Online

These days, many computer users also have access to digital cameras, Web cams or scanners, allowing them to create digital images and send them to others via email (or post the pictures on the Web).

Since chatting online involves sending text messages, it's a common practice for people to swap photos. If you choose to send your photo to a stranger you meet online, keep in mind that the photo you receive of the other person may or may not actually be that person. Also, if you're still in the closet, do you really want strangers to have a photo of you and know you're gay? Before sending a photo, you might want to get to know someone a bit better.

An alternative is to have a photo taken of yourself wearing a hat and glasses, for example, so you're not too recognizable. If you're planning on trading nude pictures of yourself with others, ask yourself if you really want pictures of your naked body floating around on the Web.

If you're openly gay, sending photos of yourself to people you meet online probably isn't too big of a deal, but use basic common sense to protect your identity and safety. When someone asks to exchange pictures, you can always say you don't have one available. Also, no matter how tempting it is, don't send out someone else's picture and say it's you. This is dishonest and disrespectful.

Web Cam Conferencing

If you have a high speed Internet connection and an inexpensive Web cam (they cost between $30.00 and $150.00), you can actually see and talk one-on-one to the people you meet online.

Using specialized software, such as Microsoft's Netmeeting (available for free from the Microsoft Web site - www.microsoft.com/windows/netmeeting), you can connect to Web servers that host online video chats. One Web cam meeting place for gay guys can be found at www.notshy.com. For a directory of servers that support meeting places for Web cam users, point your Web browser to www.netmeeting-zone.com.

Online Personals

Okay, you've probably seen personal ads that run in news-papers. People write short, sometimes hokey descriptions of themselves and the type of relationship they're looking for and hope to get responses from their ad. Well, if you're gay, there are a handful of online gay personal ad services and dating ser-vices you can use. Who knows, perhaps you'll meet Mr. Right. If you're looking to meet people, you can use an online person-al ad to pre-qualify people and find guys with similar interests. Many of these services also feature pictures with the ads, and most cost nothing to access.

If you're not brave enough to post your own personal ad, you can always check out the other guys with ads and respond to those that peak your interest. There are dozens of online per-sonal ad services for gay guys. Using any search engine, use the search phrase 'gay personals' and you'll see a list of them.

Here are a few popular Web sites that offer *free* online personal ads for young gay guys:

- Gay Café Personals - **www.gaycafe.com/personals**

- Gay Photo Ads – **www.gayphotoads.com**

- Gay Web Personals - **www.gaywebpersonals.com**

- Gay.com (Click on the 'Personals' icon) – **www.gay.com**

- PlanetOut (Click on the 'Personals' icon) – **www.planetout.com**

- XY Personals (Click on the 'Bois' icon) – **www.xymag.com**

- Yahoo! Personals - **http://personals.yahoo.com**

When creating your ad, be sure to include a catchy heading. You want someone to read the first few words of your ad and then want to read more! Keep your ad short and to the point. Describe yourself briefly and what type of relationship (or friendship) you're looking for. Remember, make yourself sound appealing.

Finding and Viewing Gay Pornography

> If you're under 18 or not into pornography, skip to the next chapter!

For those of you who are too shy (or too lazy) to visit the newsstand or video store to pick up gay porno magazines or videos, you can find just about any type of XXX-rated material online (featuring solo guys, same sex couples, groups of guys, teens, adult guys, jocks, twinks, college studs, fetishes, etc.). Most gay porn sites charge to see pictures, videos and read erotic stories. However, if you surf around a bit, you'll find an abundance of gay porn, featuring very hot guys, available for free!

While some people are totally against pornography, others get a sexual thrill from viewing it, using it to get turned on while jerking off, or simply to check out other naked guys.

Hey, if you're not too experienced when it comes to sex, checking out gay pornography might even answer some of your questions, help satisfy your curiosity or give you some ideas.

Finding gay porn on the Web is easy. Using any search engine, type in a search phrase, like 'gay porn', 'naked guys' or 'gay sex', etc., and you'll be pointed to countless Web sites. The Men On The Net Web site (**www.menonthenet.com**) is just one of many resources for finding all types of online gay pornography.

Popular Emoticons

:-) or :)

Basic Smiley
Use it to communicate sarcastic or a joking statement.

;-) or ;)

Winking Smiley
Use it to be flirtatious and/or to convey a sarcastic remark.

:-(or : (

Frowning Smiley

:-@ : @ :-O

Screaming Smiley

:-/ or : /

Skeptical Smiley

:-D

Laughing Smiley

:-o

Surprised Smiley

:-P

Sticking Out Your Tongue

Are you Addicted To The Internet?

Just as people can become addicted to alcohol, sex or drugs, more and more people are becoming addicted to the Internet. It is extremely easy to get caught up communicating for countless hours each day in the chat rooms, surfing the Web and/or viewing online pornography.

For some closeted gay teens, the Internet is their only social outlet. Like the gay club scene, this can be very alluring, and yes, addicting. So, are you addicted to the Internet?

Ask yourself these questions:

- Do you spend at least several hours each and every day surfing the Web and/or participating in chat rooms?
- Is your social life based on people you interact with online, but have never met in person?
- Have you been neglecting important family activities, social events, work responsibilities or school work to spend more time online?
- Are you using the Internet as an escape from dealing with problems you have in the real world?
- Are you not getting enough sleep at night because you stay online until the early hours of the morning?

To learn more about Internet addiction (and to take an online test to see if it applies to you), visit The Center for Online Addiction's Web site (**http://netaddiction.com**).

According to The Center for Online Addictions, "Nearly 6% of 17,251 respondents in an online survey met the criteria for compulsive Internet use and over 30% report using the Net to escape from negative feelings. The vast majority admitted to feelings of time distortion, accelerated intimacy, and feeling uninhibited when on-line."

Shout Out America

Q: Which are the popular online gay chat rooms that you're active on?

"When I first came out, I was active on the chat rooms. It was a great way to meet other gay people my age and from around the country. At the time, the chat room I used most was at PlanetOut.com."
- Christian, 15, Jupiter, FL

"I like going to TexasM4M on AOL, as well as the chat rooms on Gay.com. I met my boyfriend online about a year ago. We began chatting, then started talking via phone. After a while, we finally met in person."
- Alex, 23, McAllen, TX

"I spent time on the chat rooms when I was first coming out. It's not something I really do anymore."
- Mike, 16, Sparks, NV

"I usually hang out in the gay college rooms on AOL, as well as in the PlanetOut.com 'Youth Room.' It's fun to chat with other gay guys."
- Michael, 21, Ft. Lauderdale, FL

"I've checked out the gay-oriented chat rooms, but they don't really interest me. Most of the guys I found online just wanted to hook up."
- Josh, 18, Atlanta, GA

"Sure, I go online and chat once in a while. Typically, I'll find an AOL chat room, like CollegeJockDormM4M."
- Kyle, 19, Boulder, CO

Chapter 8

Your Life: Planning For The Future

All teenagers (not just you) have complicated lives. They're forced to juggle their personal lives at home with school work, their social schedule and possibly even a job. If you're a gay teen, the juggling act becomes far more complicated, especially if you're still in the closet and forced to lead both an openly

Photo (c) 2002 Mark V. Lynch, Latent Images

"straight" life and a secret gay life. The good news is, plenty of gay teens become expert jugglers, and despite the challenges, they prevail!

As you get older, the challenges you'll face will change. Instead of worrying about mid-term or final exams, you might become concerned about meeting deadlines at work and whether or not to come out at your workplace.

Down the road, while your peers are dealing with marital issues at home, you'll be grappling with the challenges of being in a same-sex relationship and having a domestic partner (or a 'husband'). If you choose to pursue building a family, natural childbirth with a wife is probably not in the picture, so you'll need to explore alternatives, such as adoption.

These are just some of the issues and challenges you'll face as you get older. The challenges you're facing now, whether you're in high school or college, however, tend to be more difficult. Chances are, you'll find that as you get older, the obstacles you're facing now will prepare you to deal successfully with just about anything. While your priorities and values will change over time, to achieve happiness and personal success, you'll want to lead a well-balanced life.

This chapter is divided into several parts. The first deals with how you can (and should) lead a balanced and organized life, which you control. By maintaining at least some control over your life, you'll feel less pressure and will ultimately be happier.

The latter parts of this chapter deal with issues you'll probably need to face later in life, such as pursuing a career, "getting married" (or building a strong relationship with your domestic partner) and the concept of building your own family which might someday include children.

Even if you're in high school, don't yet have a serious boyfriend, and you're still living at home, it's important to realize that your future can including everything you've dreamed about, such as a successful career and a happy family life. The fact that you're gay doesn't need to stop you from having these future objectives.

Balancing Your Life

For many people, a healthy life is divided into several distinct areas, which are broken down by how they spend their time and where their important responsibilities lie. While not all areas apply to everyone, the general areas that make up most people's lives are listed here:

- Charity Work / Volunteering
- Extracurricular Activities / Sports / Hobbies
- Family Life
- Friends
- Health & Fitness
- Religious / Spiritual
- Romance
- School
- Sleep
- Social / Entertainment
- Work

As someone gets older, the importance of each of these areas changes, as will how someone spends his time and what he considers important aspects of his life. For example, as children, most people rely heavily on their parents (or the people raising them). As kids reach their teen years, parents become less of a driving force in their lives, while someone's friends become increasingly more important, as does romance and possibily work.

A gay person's life also can be divided into distinct areas. However, added to the earlier list are additional responsibilities and time commitments, including:

- **Your Gay Life** – The time you spend online in gay chat rooms, at the gay clubs, participating in gay-oriented support group meetings, etc. If you're still closeted, this is a separate aspect of your life, with it's own time commitment(s) and responsibilities.

- **Gay Friends** – The time you spend with your gay friends. If you're still in the closet, these people might be as close as your actual family, yet kept very separate from your family and friends at school, for example.

- **Boyfriend(s)** – Instead of experiencing a typical boy/girl romance, you'll be involved in same sex relationships.

Someone who is truly a well-rounded individual will spend at least a little time in a typical day, week or month dedicating some of his attention to each area of his life. Unfortunately, few gay or straight people truly lead well-rounded lives. School work, the responsibilities of a career or romantic relationship(s) begin taking up too much time, causing them to neglect other potentially important aspects of their lives.

Right now, how much time in a typical month do you spend paying attention to each of the areas in your life? What areas of your life are being neglected? How is this neglect impacting your overall quality of life and happiness?

How Does Your Life Balance Out?

What percentage of your time in a typical week (or how many hours) is spent focusing on each of these areas of your life?

_____	Boyfriend(s)
_____	Charity Work / Volunteering
_____	Extracurricular Activities (Including: Sports & Hobbies)
_____	Family Life
_____	Friends
_____	Health & Fitness
_____	Religious / Spiritual
_____	Romance
_____	School
_____	Sleeping
_____	Social / Entertainment
_____	Work
_____	Your Gay Friends
_____	Your Gay Life

Are you a workaholic who spends too much time focusing on work or school-related responsibilities, and as a result, you don't have a personal (social) life or you don't eat properly? Are you too busy to get enough physical exercise? Are you using the fact that you have personal responsibilities to avoid pursuing a (gay-oriented) social life? Are you so caught up in the gay social scene (clubbing and partying, for example) that your school or work life is being negatively impacted?

As you go through the various stages of life, determine what's truly important to you, then do what's necessary to make time to dedicate at least some of your attention to each of those things. Every six months or once every year, spend a few minutes revaluating where your priorities lie and determine what you need to adjust in order to achieve your goals, but also lead a more balanced and well-rounded life.

One common obstacle gay people face is that their sexual orientation not only impacts their sex life, but it also becomes a driving force or obsession in other areas of their life. To an extent this is normal, especially if you've spent years in the closet and you're now coming to terms with begin gay. Being a homosexual is a part of your life – but it shouldn't be the defining factor of who you are.

Even though you're gay you can *also* be a good student, a top-notch athlete, a talented artist or musician, the hardest working employee at your job, a loving brother, a dedicated boyfriend, a loyal friend or any number of other things. Don't allow the fact that you're gay impact your ability to pursue other interests or limit what you believe you're capable of.

> Being gay doesn't have to be detrimental to your life, nor does it have to become the driving force in your life. It's your responsibility (and something you owe to yourself) to allow your life to be well-rounded, happy, productive and balanced.

In addition to dating guys (and having a romantic aspect of your life that involves men), has the fact that you're gay impacted other aspects of your life? If so, is this a good thing for you? Yes, being gay is going to require time and energy in order to deal with certain challenges and obstacles that straight people don't have to deal with. It's extremely important, however, that you stay true to the person you are (or want to be) and not allow the positive and/or negative aspects of your sexual orientation to totally consume you.

Ultimately, you could live in a gay-oriented community (such as West Hollywood, California), work for a gay or gay-friendly employer, spend your free time hanging out at the gay clubs (with only gay friends), become an active member of a gay activist group and participate in a loving relationship with a man. This life might make you totally happy. By focusing on leading the ultimate gay-oriented life, are you hiding from your fears or missing out on other potentially rewarding aspects of life? Are you alienating your family and other potentially close (straight) friends?

As you make long-term decisions that may impact the rest of your life, such as where you choose to live, what your college major will be or what type of career you'd like to pursue, think about how these decisions will impact your ability to:

- Achieve true life-long happiness
- Lead a well-rounded life
- Achieve your long-term personal, financial and career-oriented goals
- Have a loving family of your own (a domestic partner or husband)

Your Career: Working in the Straight World

You already know the gay community is plagued by countless stereotypes. When it comes to getting a job and/or pursuing a career, there are some stereotypes it's important that you, as a gay person, don't actually believe. Just because you're gay, your job (or long-term career) opportunities are *not* limited to what many perceive to be gay-oriented jobs.

You will *not* be forced to become a hairdresser, actor, work in the fashion industry or become a flight attendant, for example. Likewise, while you're still a student, your after-school or summer job doesn't need to be working for a guy's clothing store at the mall or the make-up counter of a department store. While these are all respectable jobs/careers you could pursue and be successful in, you're not at all limited to what you do for work.

Instead of worrying about pursuing a career you think will readily accept someone who's gay, choose what you *want* to do for work and what you're good at, just as everyone else does – based on your skills, education, experience and interests.

Once you know what you want to do, obtain the skills, experience and education you need to land that type of job, then find a gay-friendly employer in that field. The process is much easier than you might think!

There are many successful people in corporate America, as well as doctors, lawyers, salespeople, television producers, executive assistants, accountants, journalists, policemen, firemen, professional athletes, retail store managers and stock brokers, for example, who are gay. Some of these people stay "in the closet" at work, while others lead openly gay lives. Yet, from a career standpoint, they're successful *and* happy.

To give you an idea of how successful openly gay people can be in corporate America, check out The Gay Financial Network's Top 25 list (**www.gfn.com/gfn/gfn25.phtml**). According to the GFN, "The purpose of the list is to recognize the contributions and continued achievements of gays and lesbians who are in powerful positions, and who use those positions to make a difference on a corporate and socially responsible level." People on this list include top-level executive at companies like: AT&T, IBM, Capital One, Showtime, J.P. Morgan Chase & Co., Eastman Kodak and E*Trade.

Even if you're still in high school it's never too soon to begin exploring various career opportunities. What types of careers or jobs interest you right now? Spend some time learning about these careers, and determine what you'll ultimately need to do in order to pursue them. If you need specific training or a skill set, what's the best educational path to follow as you reach your college years?

Even if you're not sure what you'd like to pursue for a career while you're in high school or your early college years, you can still explore potential career opportunities. For example, instead of obtaining just any part-time, after-school or summer job, try landing a job (or internship) in a field that interests you. If you're 17, but know you're interested in being a lawyer, try landing a part-time job at a lawyer's office, in order to learn from firsthand experience how a law office operates.

Virtually all successful people, straight or gay, suggest to young people that they pursue internships as early in their high school or college careers as possible. Not only will you learn from an internship, you'll also obtain extremely valuable on-the-job, real-world experience (while still in school) and develop important contacts. This experience will ultimately make you a very attractive job applicant once you graduate and begin the job search process.

During your high school and college years, determine where your interests lie and figure out what types of jobs are available that will allow you to incorporate those interests into a career. Be creative! Your chances of long-term success increase dramatically if you have a true passion for the career you ultimately choose to pursue.

When it comes to your career, ask youself:

- What are your likes and dislikes?
- What are your goals and aspirations?
- What will it take to transform you into someone who is excited to wake up each and every morning and go to work?
- What do you have a passion for?
- What skills do you possess right now that make you a valuable employee?

- How can you make yourself more marketable in today's competitive job market?
- How can you incorporate your passions, hobbies, etc., into your career?

Take a few minutes and define *success* for yourself in the following areas:

My definition of professional (career-related) success is:

_____

_____

_____

_____

My definition of financial success is:

_____

_____

_____

_____

My definition of personal success is:

_____

_____

_____

_____

Once you set out to begin defining and achieving your goals, this becomes an ongoing process that requires commitment, hard work and dedication on your part. You must focus your energies and then stay focused until your objectives are fulfilled. At times this won't be an easy process, so one of the challenges you'll face is staying motivated.

The action plan you devise for achieving your goals must be personalized to meet your own needs, lifestyle and personality. You never want to take on too much, or you'll quickly find yourself overwhelmed and frustrated. Likewise, you always want to be challenged in order to maintain your interest and motivation.

In order to succeed, you'll have to determine, over time, what your personal limits are in terms of what you can handle emotionally and physically, and adjust your action plan accordingly. Most importantly, you must never be afraid to fail!

When it comes to making life-changing decisions and taking steps to improve your career, personal life or financial well being, be prepared to make mistakes, but at the same time, always learn from those mistakes and try to avoid repeating them. If you make a mistake, don't look at it as a personal failure and get depressed. Instead, consider it a valuable learning experience.

What would you do differently next time? What can be done to fix the situation now that the mistake has been made? What lessons were learned from the mistake? In the future, how can you (and how will you) benefit from the knowledge you have acquired? What can be done to insure that a similar mistake never happens again?

While hard work and dedication will play major roles in your ability to achieve long-term success, no matter what your goals are, your attitude and personality will also be integral factors. Developing and maintaining a positive attitude is important, as is learning how to work well with others so that the peo-

Photo (c) 2002 Mark V. Lynch, Latent Images

ple you work or interact with (personally or professionally) like and respect you.

Finally, always pay attention to yourself and who you are as a person. Never compromise what you believe to be moral and right simply to make someone else happy or to achieve a goal. There's always a right way and a wrong way of accomplishing something. The wrong way might save you time, money and maybe even some frustration, but in the long term, always strive to be the best person you can be.

> Once you determine the short-and long-term goals you want to achieve, invest the necessary time to create a detailed action plan so you always know what needs to be done next in order to achieve your objectives.

Yes, we're living in a highly competitive world that's filled with homophobes, liars, backstabbers, cheats and dishonest people who will do anything to get ahead. Are you one of these people? Presumably not! Do you want to become one of these people? Hopefully not! Chances are, you already know in your heart the difference between good and bad, right and wrong. Don't forget these valuable lessons you've learned as a child. Take responsibility for your actions, and take control over your own destiny.

The power to succeed is within you. Your hopes, dreams and desires can all become reality. You can make positive things happen for yourself if you're willing to take control over your own life and your actions. It's within your power to avoid getting stuck in a bad relationship and to avoid getting stuck in a dead-end job! If you're already in a bad situation, with the proper guidance and internal drive you can vastly improve and/or drastically alter the situation you're currently in.

Should You Come Out At Work?

This is a common question gay people are forced to confront whenever they apply for and ultimately accept a new job. Like everything else that relates to you and being gay, there are no easy answers.

Today, more than ever, companies in all industries and of all sizes are starting to become more gay-friendly. There's still a long way to go before gay people will be totally accepted in every type of job, so whether or not you decide to come out in the workplace is still a decision you'll be forced to make based on your own set of circumstances and what type of work you choose to pursue.

When applying for any type of job, be aware that it's illegal for a potential employer to ask if you're gay. Likewise, you're under no obligation to disclose this information when applying for a job. This includes on your job applications, on your resume or during job interviews.

As you apply for jobs and participate in job interviews, if you don't want to come out, but you're curious about the employer's policies that relate to homosexuals, you could ask generic questions to test the waters.

During the later stage of the job interview process, you might ask the interviewer about the company's diversity initiatives. Without tipping your hand, you could ask, "Can you tell me about the diversity in the workplace and related policies, as they deal with race, ethnicity, sexual orientation and the like at [insert company name]?"

At this point, there are no federal laws that protect you from being fired because you're gay (or bisexual). As of early 2002, there are, however, limited state and city laws in 12 states and approximately 30 cities. A growing number of employers, however, do have well-defined policies against discrimination based on sexual orientation.

According to The Human Rights Campaign, "At the federal level, the Human Rights Campaign is working with Congress to pass a measure called the Employment Non-Discrimination Act (ENDA). This act would prohibit discrimination based on sexual orientation. For now, however, use your best judgment when coming out at work. If you feel comfortable enough, you can be an advocate for your workplace to change its non-discrimination policy to include sexual orientation and gender identity." For more information about workplace policies and laws surrounding sexual orientation and gender identity, visit HRC's Web site at **www.hrc.org**.

From this Web site, you can download a free 36-page brochure called *State of the Workforce*, which will help you find gay-friendly employers and understand your legal rights as an employed (or soon-to-be employed) gay person.

The HRC reported that as of August 2001, the organization had identified 2,001 companies, colleges and universities, state and local governments and federal agencies that had written non-discrimination policies covering sexual orientation. This represents an increase of 293 employers, or 17 percent, in one year.

Likewise, the organization reported that 294 (or 59 percent) of the Fortune 500 companies in America included sexual orientation in their non-discrimination policies. This represented an increase of 39 companies, or 15 percent, over the prior year. "The closer a company is to the top of the Fortune 500 list, the more likely it is to have such a policy. A total of 79 percent of the Fortune 100 and 88 percent of the Fortune 50 prohibit sexual orientation discrimination," reported the HRC. Many of these companies have also begun providing benefits to domestic partners (just as they provide benefits to legally married heterosexual couples).

Ultimately, if you choose to work in the corporate world, and you're still a teenager, by the time you graduate from school and begin applying for jobs, your prospects will probably look extremely bright. As of today, the following are the top 50 most gay-friendly corporations in America, according to a study conducted by The Gay Financial Network and released on April 15, 2001:

"Chosen from among the Fortune 500 companies, each of the gfn.com 50 offers an anti-sexual-orientation-discrimination policy and same-sex domestic partners benefits. Other criteria judged by gfn.com included the companies' demonstration of financial growth and economic success, nondiscrimination on the basis of sexual orientation in the sale or purchase of goods and services, corporate policies relating to diversity training and advertising to the gay market. All 100,000 gfn.com members had the opportunity to cast a vote for the final ranking," reported The Gay Financial Network.

The Most Powerful & Gay-Friendly Public Companies in Corporate America

1. American Express Company
2. Walt Disney Company
3. Microsoft Corporation
4. Lucent Technologies
5. Xerox
6. International Business Machines (IBM)
7. Hewlett-Packard Co.
8. Apple Computer, Inc.
9. AMR Corp.
10. Citigroup, Inc.
11. Gap, Inc.
12. Verizon Communications
13. AT&T Corporation
14. AOL-Time Warner, Inc.
15. JP Morgan Chase & Co.
16. Intel Corporation
17. SBC Communications
18. Ford Motor Company
19. Compaq Computer Corporation
20. New York Times Company
21. Oracle Corporation
22. Coca-Cola Company
23. Sun Microsystems
24. Texas Instruments
25. Aetna, Inc.
26. FleetBoston Financial
27. Bank of America Corporation
28. US Airways Group, Inc.

29. General Motors Corporation
30. Boeing Company
31. Merrill Lynch & Co.
32. Charles Schwab Corporation
33. General Mills
34. Eastman Kodak Company
35. Qwest Communications International
36. UAL Corporation
37. Chevron Corporation
38. Wells Fargo & Company
39. Cisco Systems, Inc.
40. Motorola
41. Costco Wholesale Corporation
42. Chubb Corporation
43. Federated Department Stores
44. Enron Corporation (Prior to its collapse)
45. Allstate Corporation
46. Gillette Company
47. Honeywell International
48. Fannie Mae
49. Barnes & Noble, Inc.
50. Nordstrom, Inc.

Source: The Gay Financial Network, April 15, 2001

To learn more about diversity in the workplace, gay-friendly employers and the various anti-discrimination laws at the state and local level where you live, consider visiting any of these Web sites:

- Lavender Express (**www.infotycoon.com/lavenderx/careers.htm**) – This job-oriented site is ideal for gay teenagers and recent graduates. It lists full-time, part-time, seasonal and summer jobs available from gay and gay-friendly employers. It also offers an extensive listing of internship opportunities (paid and unpaid) in a wide range of industries.

- Gaywork.com (**www.gaywork.com**) – This Web site has partnered with The Monster Board (**www.Monster.com**), which is one of the Internet's most popular career-related Web sites. Gaywork.com offers nationwide job listings from gay-friendly com-

panies, plus dozens of informative articles and other
resources for gay job seekers.

■ **The Gay Financial Network (www.gfn.com)** -
Launched in 1998, the Gay Financial Network has
become a leading online resource devoted to the unique
financial needs of the gay and lesbian community.
Founded by gfn.com Chairman and CEO Walter B.
Schubert, Jr., a third-generation member and the first
openly gay member of the New York Stock Exchange,
the free site provides daily and exclusive weekly comprehensive business and financial news and information, as well as a variety of financial and investment
services specially tailored to gay and lesbian individuals and same-sex couples.

■ ProGayJobs.com – **(www.ProGayJobs.com)** – This
is another online resource for homosexual job seekers. It offers job listings, an online resume database
and many other valuable resources.

When it comes to finding great jobs and pursuing your career, being gay doesn't have to be a hindrance. In addition to
the ever growing number of Fortune 500 companies that are
gay-friendly, there are thousands of companies across America,
in virtually every industry, where you can become happily employed and have a successful career, whether you're openly gay
or choose to stay closeted.

As with every other aspect of your life, be proud of who
you are. You'll need to decide whether or not to come out in
your workplace based on your own comfort level. Make your
decision based upon where you working, the type of work you
do and the attitudes of the people you work with. Could your
sexual orientation help or hurt your professional career path
now or in the future?

Building Your Own Family

Work and your career are (or will be) important aspects of your life. After all, you'll need to pay your bills. Another important aspect of your life, however, is your family. At some point in the future, chances are you'll fall in love and want to spend the rest of your life with someone special. Perhaps you'll decide to have children and build a happy family.

While most states don't recognize gay marriages and some religions don't accept this type of union between two males, it is possible for two guys to have a binding marriage-like ceremony and lead their lives as domestic partners.

What's A Domestic Partner?

The commonly accepted definition of 'domestic partners' is two individuals who are in a long-term committed relationship and are responsi-

ble for each other's financial and emotional well-being. Employers usually set their own definitions of domestic partnership in order to determine who is eligible for domestic partner benefits. For example, you may discover that some employers require that same sex couples have lived together for at least six months, be responsible for each

Photo (c) 2002 Mark V. Lynch, Latent Images

other's financial welfare, be at least 18 years old and be mentally competent to enter into a legal contract.

The Human Rights Campaign offers these guidelines in hopes of creating a commonly accepted legal definition. At this point, however, the following are only guidelines.

For two men to be considered domestic partners, they must:

- Have lived together for a specified period (generally, at least six months)
- Be responsible for each other's financial welfare
- Not be blood relatives
- Be at least 18 years of age
- Be mentally competent
- Be life partners and would get legally married should the option become available
- Be registered as domestic partners if there is a local domestic partner registry
- Not be legally married to anyone else, including a woman
- Agree to inform the company in the event the domestic partnership terminates

On a personal level, domestic partners function the same way a married couple does. In terms of work-related employee benefits, gay-friendly companies might offer domestic partners the following benefits (just as they'd offer them to heterosexual married couples):

- Medical and dental insurance
- Disability and life insurance
- Pension benefits
- Family and bereavement leave
- Education and tuition assistance
- Credit union membership
- Relocation and travel expenses
- Inclusion of partners in company events

At this point, whether or not two gay men can "get married" and have that marriage legally recognized varies by state. Your religious faith(s) might also determine whether or not such a union can take place. Just as in corporate America, however, there is a growing acceptance of same sex relationships, so by the time you're ready to make this type of commitment, there's always a chance it could become legal in every state and/or accepted by your religion.

In the meantime, calling yourself domestic partners is not like playing make-believe. If you enter into this type of relationship, it can be as emotionally and legally binding as a real marriage, and involve the same commitments and dedication.

According to the 2000 U.S. census, approximately 600,000 same-sex couples were identified. That's more than one out of every 178 U.S. households.

Right now, there are several states, including Hawaii and Vermont, that legally recognize gay civil unions (which in many ways are just like marriages). In Vermont, this has only been the case since July 1, 2000.

Your legal rights as a couple engaged in a civil union or domestic partnership may not be recognized outside of Hawaii or Vermont. An attorney familiar with the laws relating to gay relationships and legal issues should be consulted.

Not all of the news about gay marriages, domestic partnerships or civil unions is good. Right now, in some situations, no matter what legal steps you've taken, "Under U.S. law, you are considered a total stranger to your partner in any emergency situation. If your partner should ever be knocked unconscious by an accident, in any state but Vermont, you will not be able to make any medical decisions for your partner's well being. You will not have any rights whatsoever," reports the GayWeddings.com Web site.

This Web site also reports that at this time, same sex couples do *not* share many of the same rights as married couples, including:

- Automatic visitation rights in a hospital should your partner ever get sick
- Automatic inheritance from your partner
- Being able to make medical decisions for your partner in emergencies
- Wrongful Death Benefits for the surviving partner
- Property rights and protection in the event of death
- Bereavement and sick leave rights
- Parenting and adoption
- Shared benefits like Social Security and Medicare

In Vermont, once you've worked with a lawyer to prepare for your domestic partnership or civil union (the term 'marriage' is not used), a Civil Union license can be obtained from the town clerk's office for a small fee. The Union can be certified by either a justice of the peace, a judge or a willing member of the clergy.

If you're looking to participate in a Civil Union in Vermont, one of your first steps should be to read *The Vermont Guide To Civil Unions*, published by the Office of the Secretary of State in Vermont. You can download this brochure by pointing your Web browser to **www.sec.state.vt.us/pubs/civilunions.htm**. The actual Civil Union law can be viewed at this Web site: **www.sec.state.vt.us/civilunionlaw.htm**.

Lambda Legal is a national organization committed to achieving full recognition of the civil rights of lesbians, gay men, bisexuals, the transgendered and people with HIV or AIDS through impact litigation, education and public policy work. This organization is working hard to pass laws allowing legal gay marriages (or similar legally binding ceremonies) is every state in America. For information on the specific laws in your state, point your Web browser to: **www.lambdalegal.org/cgi-bin/iowa/states** or call **(212) 809-8585**.

Lambda's Web site offers an excellent resource for same-sex couples looking to get married, form a domestic partnership or civil union and deal with the legal issues surrounding these.

You do not need to live in Hawaii or Vermont to participate in a legal domestic partnership or civil union ceremony. By having a legal ceremony and taking a few basic legal steps, you can obtain some of the legal rights not automatically given to you. For example, you'll want to work with a lawyer to create a Living Will and Power of Attorney documents.

According to Lambda, couples who wish legal recognition for their marriage must first get a license issued by the government and then have an authorized person marry them. This is a civil marriage. Depending on the state, the person who marries the couple may be a government official (such as a justice of the peace or city hall official) or an otherwise authorized individual (such as some clergy).

But if the couple asks a clergyperson to marry them, that clergyperson can always say no, meaning that the couple would have to ask some other authorized person.

- Religious groups retain the right to marry or not to marry couples, as they wish, according to their religious principles.

- Though many faiths do perform marriage ceremonies for same-sex couples, at present these marriages have no legal recognition because they have not been licensed by the government, and thus are not *civil* marriages.

- Religions should not dictate who gets a marriage license from the state, just as the state should not dictate which marriage any religion performs or recognizes.

In addition to a civil union or domestic partnership, some same-sex couples have begun setting up their own limited liability partnerships to give themselves additional legal rights as a couple. For information about this, visit the Relationship LLC Web site at **www.relationshipllc.com**. There are many legal ramifications to this, so be sure to contact a lawyer.

Okay, once you've gotten through all of the legal stuff relating to a civil union or domestic partnership, it's time for the romantic stuff, like proposing, choosing rings and planning a ceremony. All of these things happen in much the same way as a straight couple getting engaged and married. Make the event something special – that you'll remember for a lifetime!

If you're looking for beautiful, hand-crafted platinum, gold, diamond or titanium wedding bands, visit any local jewelry store or check out these Web sites:
www.Titaniumera.com
www.Diamonds.com
www.GayMart.com

Open Relationships

One way gay couples build their relationships is to work together toward satisfying all of their emotional and physical needs. In some instances, when the two partners don't totally fulfil each other's needs, they sometimes consider having an 'open relationship.'

This can have many meanings and impact a relationship in a variety of ways. After setting specific ground rules (which both partners agree to in advance), either a third person is brought into the bedroom as a sex partner (to add variety), or the partners in the relationship might agree to allow each other to have sexual relations with other men, without it being considered cheating.

This type of arrangement is certainly not suitable for everyone. However, for some couples, it keeps the sexual aspect of the relationship exciting and fresh, while allowing the couple to continue sharing their strong emotional and loving bond or partnership.

Participation in an open relationship takes a tremendous level of trust, respect and love. While there are many potential things that can cause this type of relationship to fail, for some gay couples, having an open relationship makes it possible for two people who are in love to stay together without sneaking behind their partner's back to cheat, for example.

Whether or not participating in this type of relationship is right for you is based upon your own personal situation as well as your morals, values and feelings toward your boyfriend or partner.

Choosing to have an open relationship doesn't necessarily make your relationship any less loving or valid than anyone else's.

Planning To Be A Parent?

Whether or not you decide to participate in a civil union, domestic partnership or gay marriage, at some point in your life you may choose to raise children.

There are many different ways gay men can do this, including adoption. The laws pertaining to adoption vary by state, so you'll want to consult with adoption agencies and lawyers to learn more. You also have the option to become a foster parent and help children in need.

According to the American Civil Liberties Union, in the past ten years, there has been a sharp rise in the number of gay men forming their own families through adoption, foster care, artificial insemination and other means. As of 1999, researchers estimate the total number of children nationwide living with at least one gay parent ranges from six to 14 million.

The following are a few online resources to help you learn about the ways you, as a gay male, can build your own family:

- The American Civil Liberties Union
  www.aclu.org/issues/gay/parent.html

- Adopting.org
  www.adopting.org

- The Gay Adoption Mailing List
  http://maelstrom.stjohns.edu/archives/gay-aparent.html

- Gay Parent Magazine
  www.gayparentmag.com

Gay Activisim

For many, being gay is something they're proud of and open about. For the general public to better understand the gay community and to help fight the common and inaccurate misconceptions of homosexuality, it takes people to actively work toward educating the public, rally to create and pass anti-discrimination laws and other laws (that protect the rights of gay people everywhere) and to help curb the homophobic attitudes too many straight people still have.

Photo (c) 2002 Mark V. Lynch, Latent Images

If and when you're ready to take an active role in any of these activities, there are countless groups you can volunteer your time with to work toward making a difference. Even if you don't have any desire to be a gay activist, just by leading your life you can show the world that gay people are normal, friendly and caring people. Instead of working to promote the gay stereotypes, you can work in your own subtle way to break those stereotypes – even if it's just among your family members and close friends.

When a straight person sees you're gay, but that you don't fit any of their negative stereotypes, you've taken a step toward educating someone else, just by leading your life and setting an example. Nobody should tell you how to lead your life, but as a gay teenager, the way you act in public (around straight people) and the success you achieve in your life will all contribute to the positive image of homosexuality and impact the way the gay community as a whole is perceived. Be mindful of other people, but be yourself!

Just because you're gay, you're in no way obligated to be the gay poster boy in your community. If you're openly gay, however, consider taking part in local Gay Pride events or be willing to answer the questions posed by straight people around you.

If you choose to be a voice in the gay community, think about the ramications of your actions so you don't jeopardize your own safety trying to communicate a message ome people simply don't want to hear.

Photo (c) 2002 Mark V. Lynch, Latent Images

By Becoming A Gay Activist
You Can Make A Difference!

If you want to make a difference, here are just some of the hundreds of gay rights organizations you can join and become a gay activist:

- Act Up
  www.actup.org

- AIDS Action Committee
  www.aac.org

- American Civil Liberties Union
  www.aclu.org/issues/gay/hmgl.html

- Gay & Lesbian Activists Alliance
  www.glaa.org

- Gay-Straight Alliance Network
  www.gsanetwork.org

- Lambda
  www.lambdalegal.org

- National Freedom To Marry Coalition
  www.freedomtomarry.org

- PFLAG
  www.pflag.org

- Rainbow Query
  www.rainbowquery.com

- Scouting For All
  www.scoutingforall.org

- The P.E.R.S.O.N. Project
  www.youth.org/loco/PERSONProject

- Youth Assistance Organization
  www.youth.org

Shout Out America
Q: Have you come out at work? Why or why not?

"Yes, but not to a point that it bothers people. Being gay is one aspect of my life - it's not my entire life."
- Michael, 21, Ft. Lauderdale, FL

"No, not at all. It's none of their business!"
- Alex, 23, McAllen, TX

"Yes. I am often very vocal, even about my sex life. My coworkers always ask me questions and are often left intrigued by my stories."
- Tristan, 19, Los Angeles, CA

"At first, I kept my sexuality to myself. It was nobody's business. As I got to know my coworkers, however, I gradually filled them in. I wanted to make sure my being gay wouldn't jeorpardize my job or damage my professional reputation."
- Scott, 25, New York, NY

"I work at one of those popular retail guys' clothing stores at the mall. I'm surrounded by other gay coworkers around my age."
- Peter, 18, Boston, MA

Chapter 9

Homosexuality vs. Religion

Living and Working In The Straight World

Once you come out to your close friends and family, you must still decide if you want to lead an openly gay life or keep your sexuality a secret from the people at school, work and in your everyday life.

Depending on where you go to school or work, for example, the environment may or may not be gay friendly. Thus, to fit in better, you may choose to act 'straight'.

Do you think you're convincing what you try acting straight? The Straight Acting Web site (**www.straightacting.com/guyquiz.shtml**) offers a fun and comical quiz. Try testing yourself.

Obviously, dating a girl is an excellent cover, but before you do this, think carefully about the ramifications. If you choose to date a girl simply as a cover, you run the definite risk of hurting that person. Imagine being a girl and finding out the guy you're in love with not only doesn't love you, but is gay and never loved you. That can be emotionally devastating.

Whether or not you truly have feelings for your 'girlfriend' (romantic or otherwise), if you're knowingly using her to cover up your homosexuality (and she doesn't know the real situation), that's wrong. If you're cheating on your girlfriend (because you're also in a secret relationship with a guy), this too isn't right. It's selfish and could lead to problems.

Some high school guys who are involved in relationships with girls discover along the way their interests lie elsewhere. This is another story altogether. Your teen years are a time of discovery, exploration and growth. If you're in a wonderful relationship with a female (and you're both happy), but you begin questioning your sexuality, don't ignore your feelings, but don't act rashly either. Eventually, however, you'll have to make a decision, and pick your team, so to speak.

Going through a period of questioning and/or sexual confusion during your teen years and being gay or bisexual are very different things. Even if you choose to act on your homosexual feelings, you may discover you still like girls and that you're either bisexual or totally straight (but had some natural and normal curiosity).

This chapter deals with the subject of religion and personal faith. It is meant to provide general guidance in helping someone come to terms with their sexuality and religious beliefs. It is in no way meant to offend anyone or denounce or disrespect any religion or spiritual belief system.

One of the least understood aspects of homosexuality is how it relates to religion. Most well-established and organized religions have a negative stance on homosexuality, yet at the same time preach about love and acceptance of everyone. When it comes to religion and homosexuality, contradictions appear to be the norm. Yet, by staying true to your personal faith and beliefs, whatever religion you believe in, you can find fulfillment in the spiritual aspect of your life.

Some religions now accept or at least acknowledge homosexuality, and preach that being gay isn't a sin. As a gay male, your sexual orientation, however, may be a sin in the eyes of your religious leaders. A lot comes down to what religion you affiliate yourself with, what your personal belief system is and how you (and your religious leaders) choose to interpret the Bible and/or other holy scriptures.

re·li·gion - **1 a :** the state of a religious <a nun in her 20th year of *religion*> **b** (1) : the service and worship of God or the supernatural (2) : commitment or devotion to religious faith or observance **2 :** a personal set or institutionalized system of religious attitudes, beliefs, and practices **3** *archaic* : scrupulous conformity : CONSCIENTIOUSNESS
4 : a cause, principle, or system of beliefs held to with ardor and faith - **re·li·gion·less** *adjective*.

(Source: Merriam-Webster Collegiate Dictionary, **www.m-w.com**)

If your religion denounces homosexuality, then you'll be forced to make an important decision that will impact many aspects of your life. Should you be true to the religion you were brought up with, or true to the person you know in your heart you are? Is it specific religious leaders or organized religions that don't accept you, or is it your personal belief that the God you believe in won't accept you as a gay male? These are questions nobody can answer for you, nor are they questions you can answer without giving them a tremendous amount of consideration.

When it comes to the ramifications of accepting your sexual orientation and a religious affiliation, the best advice is to seek guidance from others, including your parents, gay friends and religious leaders.

Like all religions, the Catholic Church has its own stand on homosexuality. The following is an excerpt from a document entitled, *"The Pontifical Council for the Family: The Truth and Meaning of Human Sexuality, Guidelines for Education within the Family,"* published by the Vatican (**www.vatican.va**):

"A particular problem that can appear during the process of sexual maturation is *homosexuality*, which is also spreading more and more in urbanized societies. This phenomenon must be presented with balanced judgment, in the light of the documents of the Church. Young people need to be helped to distinguish between the concepts of what is normal and abnormal, between subjective guilt and objective disorder, avoiding what would arouse hostility. On the other hand, the structural and complementary orientation of sexuality must be well clarified in relation to marriage, procreation and Christian chastity. 'Homosexuality refers to relations between men or between women who experience an exclusive or predominant sexual attraction toward persons of the same sex. It has taken a great variety of forms through the centuries and in different cultures. Its psychological genesis remains largely unexplained'. A distinction must be made between a tendency that can be innate and acts of homosexuality that 'are intrinsically disordered' and contrary to Natural Law.

"Especially when the practice of homosexual acts has not become a habit, many cases can benefit from appropriate therapy. In any case, persons in this situation must be accepted with respect, dignity and delicacy, and all forms of unjust discrimination must be avoided. If parents notice the appearance of this tendency or of related behavior in their children, during childhood or adolescence, they should seek help from expert qualified persons in order to obtain all possible assistance.

"For most homosexual persons, this condition constitutes a trial. 'They must be accepted with respect, compassion and sensitivity. Every sign of unjust discrimination in their regard should be avoided. These persons are called to fulfill God's will in their lives and, if they are Christians, to unite to the sacrifice of the Lord's Cross the difficulties they may encounter from their condition'. 'Homosexual persons are called to chastity'."

Chas·ti·ty - 1 : the quality or state of being chaste: as **a :** abstention from unlawful sexual intercourse **b :** abstention from all sexual intercourse **c :** purity in conduct and intention **d :** restraint and simplicity in design or expression **2 :** personal integrity.
(Source: Merriam-Webster Collegiate Dictionary, **www.m-w.com**)

Based on this document, it would appear (although it's probably subject to interpretation), that the Catholic Church is asking its homosexual followers to either accept its beliefs, but forfeit their sexual orientation, or vice-versa. By going against the Catholic Church in order to live your life as a homosexual male (assuming you're Catholic and gay, of course), are you turning against God, or just the beliefs of the religious leaders running the church? Again, this is a determination that you must make for yourself, hopefully, by seeking the guidance of others.

Dignity USA (**800-877-8797 / www.dignityusa.org**) is just one of many organizations designed to help Catholics come to terms with both their religion and sexual orientation. According to this organization, "We believe that gay, lesbian, bisexual and transgender Catholics in our diversity are members of Christ's mystical body, numbered among the People of God.

We have an inherent dignity because God created us, Christ died for us, and the Holy Spirit sanctified us in Baptism, making us temples of the Spirit, and channels through which God's love becomes visible. Because of this, it is our right, our privilege, and our duty to live the sacramental life of the Church, so that we might become more powerful instruments of God's love working among all people.

"We believe that gay, lesbian, bisexual and transgender persons can express their sexuality in a manner that is consonant with Christ's teaching. We believe that we can express our sexuality physically, in a unitive manner that is loving, life-giving, and life-affirming. We believe that all sexuality should be exercised in an ethically responsible and unselfish way. DIGNITY is organized to unite gay, lesbian, bisexual and transgender Catholics, as well as our families, friends and loved ones in order to develop leadership, and be an instrument through which we may be heard by and promote reform in the Church."

This is just one of many other points of view, as it relates to the Catholic Church and homosexuality.

Religion Versus Spirituality

Many gay teenagers feel burned by organized religion. Despite their personal belief and faith, they are turned away or snubbed because of their sexual orientation. Some gay people never come out, simply because their religion frowns upon it. While you may or may not choose to associate yourself with an organized religion, it's still possible to become a highly spiritual person.

The books, *What The Bible Really Says About Homosexuality* by Daniel A. Helminiak, PH.D. (Alamo Square Press, $14.00) and *Gay Spirituality : The Role of Gay Identity in the Transformation of Human Consciousness* by Edwin Clark Johnson and Toby Johnson (Alyson Publications, $26.90) are excellent resources for someone questioning their religious faith as they come to terms with their sexual orientation. As you'll see in the next section, there are also religious organizations, including churches and temples, that welcome gay members.

Whatever your religious faith is, the following are some useful resources to help you find the religious guidance you may choose to seek out:

Religious Organizations

Nobody can force you to be religious or adopt a set of ideologies or beliefs. You must seek out and embrace whatever religious or spiritual guidance you're comfortable with, from individuals and/or religious organizations that you choose to support and that choose to support you.

The following is a listing of religious organizations, encompassing many faiths, which support the gay community. This list is included here as a resource, but is not intended to be an endorsement of any or all of the organizations' beliefs and/or practices. As you seek to find spiritual and religious fulfillment in your life, you may choose to learn more about what these organizations offer.

Affirmation (Mormon)
P.O. Box 46022
Los Angeles, CA 90046-0022
(323) 255-7251 / www.affirmation.org

Integrity (Episcopalian)
1718 M St., N.W.
Washington, DC 20036
(202) 462-9193 / www.integrityusa.org

Affirmation (United Methodist)
P.O. Box 1021
Evanston, IL 60204
(847) 733-9590 / www.umaffirm.org

Lutherans Concerned
P.O. Box 1022
Indianapolis, IN 46206-1922
www.lcna.org

More Light Presbyterians
369 Montezuma Ave., #447
Santa Fe, NM 87501-2626
(505) 820-7082 / www.mlp.org

Al-Fatiha Foundation (Muslim)
405 Park Ave., Ste. 1500
New York, NY 10022
(212) 752-4242 / www.al-fatiha.net

Brethren/Mennonite Council for Lesbian and Gay Concerns
P.O. Box 6300
Minneapolis, MN 55406
(612) 722-6906
www.webcom.com/bmc/welcome.html

Office of GLBT Concerns for Unitarian Universalists Association
25 Beacon Street
Boston, MA 02108
(617) 948-6475 / www.uua.org/obgltc
Dignity/USA (Catholic)
1500 Massachusetts Ave., N.W.,
Ste. 11
Washington, DC 20005-1894
(800) 877-8797 / www.dignityusa.org

SDA Kinship International (Seventh-Day Adventist)
P.O. Box 7320
Laguna Niguel, CA 92607
(949) 248-1299 / www.sdakinship.org

Jason R. Rich

United Fellowship of Metropolitan Community Churches
8704 Santa Monica Blvd., 2nd Floor
West Hollywood, CA 90069
(310) 360-8640 / www.ufmcc.com

Evangelicals Concerned with Reconciliation
P.O. Box 19734
Seattle, WA 98109-6734
(206)621-8960 / www.ecwr.org

World Congress of Gay and Lesbian Jewish Organizations
P.O. Box 23379
Washington, DC 20026-3379
(202) 452-7424 / www.wcgljo.org

Gay Buddhist Fellowship
2215-R Market St., Ste. 162
San Francisco, CA 94114
(415) 207-8113 / www.gaybuddhist.org

Unity Fellowship Church Movement
(African American)
5148 West Jefferson Blvd.
Los Angeles, CA 90016
(323) 938-8322 / www.unityfellowshipchurch.org

BeliefNet (www.belief.net / AOL Keyword: Faith Finder) is a multi-faith e-community offering informative articles and interactive discussions on a wide range of topics pertaining to spirituality and religion. There's even an online quiz to help you determine which religion best fits with your personal beliefs, plus there's an area of this site specifically for teens. No matter what religion you belong to or where your faith lies, this is an inspirational Web site that's well worth checking out.

Shout Out America

Q: How have you dealt with the religious ramifications of being gay? Whom have you sought guidance from?

"I figure the only one to judge me is Jesus Christ and all other 'religious' people who try to judge me can mind their own business. My religion teacher has been very helpful. He truly understands, because his daughter is gay."
- Joseph, 21, Windsor Locks, CT

"I'm not very religious and I am still dealing with the ramifications of how religion and my sexuality fit into my life. I have a pastor whom I consider to be my 'dad', so that helps."
- Alex, 23, McAllen, TX

"I'm not religious, but I'm spiritual. I lost my faith in organized religion after I was told I was going to hell like eight million times. I stopped going to church. I do, however, believe there's a higher power of some sort."
- Adam, 21, Lovington, IL

"I believe in God and I am Catholic, but I don't go to church. I'm not really proud to be gay, but it's who I am and I am starting to accept it."
- Kyle, 18, Boulder, CO

"I was born Jewish and consider myself spiritual, but I don't follow the teachings of any organized religion. I believe in God and I pray, but in my own way. I am totally at peace with that. I know God understands me and my sexuality, and wants me to be happy."
- David, 22, Boise, ID

"My God doesn't discriminate against age, sex or sexual orientation. At first, I looked to my mother for religious guidance, but I soon realized we believed different things."
- Josh, 18, Atlanta, GA

I don't think any one religion is right. I am a very spiritual person. My spiritual friend provides me with a lot of insight and guidance."
- Tristan, 19, Los Angeles, CA

Now, That's Entertainment!
Gay-Oriented Movie Suggestions: Take 3

The following are additional movies with gay-oriented storylines and/or themes that are available on VHS and DVD from Picture This Home Video (**888-604-8301 / www.picturethisent.com**) and other video stores and rental locations. Some of these films contain strong language, nudity and/or deal with controversial issues.

- **Come Undone** - While on a family vacation, 18-year-old Mathieu meets Cédric, an attractive, carefree boy his own age. Together, they are swept away by the stirrings of homosexual passion. Subtitled French film. (Not Rated, Picture This Entertainment, 2000)

- **The Toilers and the Wayfarers** - Dieter and his friend Philip are trapped in a small town that is slowly suffocating them. Both boys are frightened by their emerging sexual identities, but at sixteen, simmering passions are easy to ignite, especially when they are fueled by each other's touch. (Not Rated, Outsider Enterprises, 1997)

- **From The Edge of the City** - 17-year-old Sasha is the leader of a gang of Greek kids who live precariously on the margins of Athens, hustling by night in Omonia Square. Having come with their families from Kazakhstan as refugees, they are shunned in their new homeland, even though they are ethnic Greeks. With drugs fueling their increasingly volatile existence, their lives and the ties that bind them eventually shatter as they collide with the city's harsh underside. Subtitled. (Not Rated, Picture This! Entertainment, 2000)

- **Eban and Charlie** - Eban, a 29-year-old ex-soccer coach meets Charley, a 15 year-old with whom he shares similar interests. The two also commiserate over similarly uneasy home lives. After a day spent playing music and walking on the beach, their friendship leads to a deeper emotional intimacy that they both desperately need. The two must decide whether to continue their relationship or risk their families' (and society's) condemnation. (Not Rated, Picture This! Entertainment, 2000)

About The Author

Jason R. Rich is a newspaper and magazine columnist. He's also the author of more than 25 books on a wide range of topics, including: career-related issues, the Internet, travel, computer/video games, the paranormal, organization, goal setting and surviving college.

Jason lives outside of Boston. You can email him directly at **jr7777@aol.com** or visit this book's Web site at **www.Growing-Up-Gay.com**.

About The Photographer

Mark V. Lynch is the president of Latent Images Photography in Austin, Texas. He's been working as a professional photographer for over 20 years.

"The models I shoot are not professionals. Without their talent and dedication, my work would not be possible," states Mark.

If you enjoyed the photos of the hot guys throughout this book, you can thank Mark for so generously providing them. Want to see more? Be sure to check out his Web site at **www.latentimages.com**. You can also email Mark at **mark@latentimages.com**. (Sorry, he won't give out the models' phone numbers.)

Check out this book's official Web site at:
www.Growing-Up-Gay.com

Ur Attention please

Interested in a cozy, cute, predictable magazine with attractive pictures of phytoplankton?

YOU ARE?

Then you can

DETONATE THIS MAG

Because XY, the world's best-selling gay youth magazine, is way too dope for the likes of YOU! If, however...

STURGEON GENENERALS WARNING!— Just do NOT get out of your bed without <u>XY.Com</u> and <u>XY Magazine</u> every month! <u>Why?</u> Cause it's the biggest best young gay magazine and website in the <u>universe</u>!

POLITICS-10000 PERSONALS-Club guide to EVERYWHERE-coming out-LOTS OF HOT BOYS-music games books and film-LIFE

It's all at XY.Com! Yay!

Hey! XY Magazine is <u>at your local bookstore</u> each month too!

3M

Printed in the United States
779300003B